Seeds of Contemplation

THOMAS MERTON

Originally published as
New Seeds of Contemplation

ANTHONY CLARKE BOOKS
Wheathampstead, Hertfordshire

Nihil Obstat: James F. Rigney, S.T.D., Censor Librorum
Imprimatur: ✠Francis Cardinal Spellman, Archbishop of New York

Ex parte Ordinis

Nihil Obstat   Fr. M. Paul Bourne, O.C.S.O.
                Fr. M. Thomas Aquinas Porter, O.C.S.O.
Imprimi Potest: Fr. M. Gabriel Sortais, Abbot General
April 10, 1961

TU QUI SEDES IN TENEBRIS

SPE TUA GAUDE:

ORTA STELLA MATUTINA

SOL NON TARDABIT

SBN 85650 023 2

© COPYRIGHT, 1961, BY THE ABBEY OF OUR LADY OF GETHSEMANI

First published in Great Britain 1962, under title
New Seeds of Contemplation by Burns & Oates Ltd.
Paperback edition 1972
Anthony Clarke Books
Wheathampstead, Hertfordshire
Made and printed in Great Britain by
Robert MacLehose and Co Ltd, The University Press, Glasgow

Contents

PREFACE V

AUTHOR'S NOTE viii

1 WHAT IS CONTEMPLATION? 1

2 WHAT CONTEMPLATION IS NOT 5

3 SEEDS OF CONTEMPLATION 12

4 EVERYTHING THAT IS, IS HOLY 17

5 THINGS IN THEIR IDENTITY 23

6 PRAY FOR YOUR OWN DISCOVERY 29

7 UNION AND DIVISION 37

8 SOLITUDE IS NOT SEPARATION 41

9 WE ARE ONE MAN 50

10 A BODY OF BROKEN BONES 55

11 LEARN TO BE ALONE 62

12 THE PURE HEART 65

13 THE MORAL THEOLOGY OF THE DEVIL 69

14 INTEGRITY 75

15 SENTENCES 80

16 THE ROOT OF WAR IS FEAR 86

17 HELL AS HATRED 95

18 FAITH 98

19 FROM FAITH TO WISDOM 102

20 TRADITION AND REVOLUTION 111

21 THE MYSTERY OF CHRIST 117

22 LIFE IN CHRIST 123

23 THE WOMAN CLOTHED WITH THE SUN 130

24 HE WHO IS NOT WITH ME IS AGAINST ME 137

CONTENTS

25 HUMILITY AGAINST DESPAIR 140

26 FREEDOM UNDER OBEDIENCE 149

27 WHAT IS LIBERTY? 155

28 DETACHMENT 158

29 MENTAL PRAYER 166

30 DISTRACTIONS 171

31 THE GIFT OF UNDERSTANDING 174

32 THE NIGHT OF THE SENSES 181

33 JOURNEY THROUGH THE WILDERNESS 185

34 THE WRONG FLAME 190

35 RENUNCIATION 194

36 INWARD DESTITUTION 203

37 SHARING THE FRUITS OF CONTEMPLATION 208

38 PURE LOVE 214

39 THE GENERAL DANCE 225

Preface

THIS is not merely a new edition of an old book. It is in many ways a completely new book. The full substance of the former work has been retained, only a sentence here and there has been discarded. Minor corrections have been made in the original text, and there have been very numerous additions. Almost every chapter has been considerably expanded and several completely new chapters have been added. The purpose of this revision was not simply to make a larger book out of a small one, but to say many new things that could profitably be added to the old. And there was very good reason for saying these new things within the context of what was said before, in a different way.

More than twelve years have passed between the first and second redactions of this text. When the book was first written, the author had no experience in confronting the needs and problems of other men. The book was written in a kind of isolation, in which the author was alone with his own experience of the contemplative life. And such a book can be written best, perhaps only, in solitude. The second writing has been no less solitary than the first: but the author's solitude has been modified by contact with other solitudes; with the loneliness, the simplicity, the perplexity of novices and scholastics of his monastic community; with the loneliness of people outside any monastery; with the loneliness of people outside the Church. . . .

As a result of this new perspective, many questions confronted the writer on taking up this old work again. Not least was the very use of the word *contemplation*. It is a misleading word in many respects. It raises great hopes that are all too likely to be illusory because misunderstood. It can become almost a magic word, or if not magic, then inspirational, which is almost as bad.

But the worst disadvantage of the word is that it sounds like "something," an objective quality, a spiritual commodity that one can procure, something that it is good to have; something which, when possessed, liberates one from problems and from unhappiness. As if there were a new project to be undertaken, among all the million other projects suggested to us in our lifetime: to become contemplatives.

One of the things that was misleading about the earlier version of this work is that it seemed to teach the reader "how to become a contemplative." That was not the author's intention, because it is impossible for one man to teach another "how to become a contemplative." One might as well write a book: "How to be an angel."

To refuse to use the word *contemplation* would make the task of revision impossible. So the book has been revised in its own original terms. Explanations have been added, and the first two chapters of the new book are devoted to some descriptive notes on the contemplative experience which the reader will peruse at his own risk.

The first version of the book, without intending to be popular, was read by many. It does not matter whether or not many read the second version, so long as it reaches some of the few for whom it is intended. It is not intended for everybody. It is not intended for all religious people. It is not addressed primarily to Catholics, though it should be clear that the author has tried, in every case, to explain difficult matters in language that accords with Catholic theology.

There are very many religious people who have no need for a book like this, because theirs is a different kind of spirituality. If to them this book is without meaning, they should not feel concerned. On the other hand, there are perhaps people without formal religious affiliations who will find in these pages something that appeals to them. If they do, I am glad, as I feel myself a debtor to them more than to the others.

PUBLISHER'S NOTE TO NEW EDITION

At the author's request the word NEW is deleted from the title of this work. The original Seeds of Contemplation is now out of print but this present book retains the full substance of the earlier work and almost every chapter has been extended. There are also many additional chapters.

Author's Note

THIS is the kind of book that writes itself almost automatically in a monastery. Perhaps that is one reason why relatively few such books get written. There is too much passion and too much physical violence for men to want to reflect much on the interior life and its meaning. Yet since the interior life and contemplation are the things we most of all need—I speak only of contemplation that springs from the love of God—the kind of considerations written in these pages ought to be something for which everybody, and not only monks, would have a great hunger in our time. And that is why I think a volume of more or less disconnected thoughts and ideas and aphorisms about the interior life needs no particular apology or excuse, even though this kind of book may have become unfamiliar.

If the reader needs any reminder that there exists a long tradition of such writing, he may consult Pascal's *Pensées*, the *Cautelas* and *Avisos* of St. John of the Cross, the *Meditationes* of Guigo the Carthusian, or, for that matter, the *Imitation of Christ*. But since to mention such names would seem to suggest a comparison with the work of great men whom the author would never dare to imitate, he simply mentions them to justify the publication of what is nothing more than a collection of notes and personal reflections.

These are the kind of thoughts that might have occurred to any Cistercian monk;* they came to mind at odd moments

---

*In the twelve years since this was written and published, not a few Cistercians have vehemently denied that these thoughts were either characteristic or worthy of a normal Cistercian, which is perhaps quite true.

and were put down on paper when there was time, without order and without any special sequence. They do not cover everything in the interior life. On the contrary, much is assumed or presupposed. Everything taught in the Gospel of Christ and the Rule of St. Benedict, everything accepted by Catholic tradition about the self-discipline of Christian asceticism is here taken for granted, and there is no attempt at apologetics on these points or any others. Much of what is said has its origin and justification in the writings of the Cistercians of the twelfth century, especially those of St. Bernard of Clairvaux, who did most to form the spirituality of the contemplative Order to which the author belongs. But those who have made the acquaintance of St. John of the Cross will find that much that is said about contemplative prayer follows lines laid down by the Spanish Carmelite. And so this book makes no claim to be revolutionary or even especially original. We sincerely hope it does not contain a line that is new to Christian tradition.

And that is why the book could have been written by any monk. It expresses the preoccupations that are more or less in the minds of all contemplatives—allowing for differences of temperament and personality. It has no other end or ideal in view than what should be the ordinary fulfilment of the Christian life of grace, and therefore everything that is said here can be applied to anyone, not only in the monastery but also in the world.

The book does not claim, either, to be a work of art. Practically anybody else with the same interests might possibly have written it much better. The fact that this author happens to have written it does not make much difference one way or the other, either for better or, we hope, for worse. For this is the kind of book that achieves an effect that is not and cannot be controlled by any human author. If you can bring yourself, somehow, to read it in communion with the God in whose Presence it was written, it will interest you and you will probably draw some fruit from it, more by His grace than by the author's efforts. But if you cannot read it under these conditions, no doubt the book will be at least a novelty.

1

What is Contemplation?

CONTEMPLATION is the highest expression of man's intellectual and spiritual life. It is that life itself, fully awake, fully active, fully aware that it is alive. It is spiritual wonder. It is spontaneous awe at the sacredness of life, of being. It is gratitude for life, for awareness and for being. It is a vivid realization of the fact that life and being in us proceed from an invisible, transcendent and infinitely abundant Source. Contemplation is, above all, awareness of the reality of that Source. It *knows* the Source, obscurely, inexplicably, but with a certitude that goes both beyond reason and beyond simple faith. For contemplation is a kind of spiritual vision to which both reason and faith aspire, by their very nature, because without it they must always remain incomplete. Yet contemplation is not vision because it sees "without seeing" and knows "without knowing." It is a more profound depth of faith, a knowledge too deep to be grasped in images, in words or even in clear concepts. It can be suggested by words, by symbols, but in the very moment of trying to indicate what it knows the contemplative mind takes back what it has said, and denies what it has affirmed. For in contemplation we know by "unknowing." Or, better, we know *beyond* all knowing or "unknowing."

Poetry, music and art have something in common with the contemplative experience. But contemplation is beyond aesthetic intuition, beyond art, beyond poetry. Indeed, it is also beyond philosophy, beyond speculative theology. It resumes, transcends and fulfils them all, and yet at the same time it seems, in a certain way, to supersede and to deny them all. Contemplation is always beyond our own knowledge, beyond our own light, beyond systems, beyond explanations, beyond discourse, beyond dialogue, beyond our own self. To enter into the realm of contemplation one must in a certain sense die: but this death is in fact the entrance into a higher life. It is a death for the sake of life, which leaves behind all that we can know or treasure as life, as thought, as experience, as joy, as being.

And so contemplation seems to supersede and to discard every other form of intuition and experience—whether in art, in philosophy, in theology, in liturgy or in ordinary levels of love and of belief. This rejection is of course only apparent. Contemplation is and must be compatible with all these things, for it is their highest fulfilment. But in the actual experience of contemplation all other experiences are momentarily lost. They "die" to be born again on a higher level of life.

In other words, then, contemplation reaches out to the knowledge and even to the experience of the transcendent and inexpressible God. It knows God by seeming to touch Him. Or rather it knows Him as if it had been invisibly touched by Him. . . . Touched by Him who has no hands, but who is pure Reality and the source of all that is real! Hence contemplation is a sudden gift of awareness, an awakening to the Real within all that is real. A vivid awareness of infinite Being at the roots of our own limited being. An awareness of our contingent reality as received, as a present from God, as a free gift of love. This is the existential contact of which we speak when we use the metaphor of being "touched by God."

Contemplation is also the response to a call: a call from Him who has no voice, and yet who speaks in everything that is, and who, most of all, speaks in the depths of our own being:

for we ourselves are words of His. But we are words that are meant to respond to Him, to answer to Him, to echo Him, and even in some way to contain Him and signify Him. Contemplation is this echo. It is a deep resonance in the inmost centre of our spirit in which our very life loses its separate voice and re-sounds with the majesty and the mercy of the Hidden and Living One. He answers Himself in us and this answer is divine life, divine creativity, making all things new. We ourselves become His echo and His answer. It is as if in creating us God asked a question, and in awakening us to contemplation He answered the question, so that the contemplative is, at the same time, question and answer.

THE life of contemplation implies two levels of awareness: first, awareness of the question, and second, awareness of the answer. Though these are two distinct and enormously different levels, yet they are in fact an awareness of the same thing. The question is, itself, the answer. And we ourselves are both. But we cannot know this until we have moved into the second kind of awareness. We awaken, not to find an answer absolutely distinct from the question, but to realize that the question is its own answer. And all is summed up in one awareness—not a proposition, but an experience: "I AM."

The contemplation of which I speak here is not philosophical. It is not the static awareness of metaphysical essences apprehended as spiritual objects, unchanging and eternal. It is not the contemplation of abstract ideas. It is the religious apprehension of God, through my life in God, or through "sonship" as the New Testament says. "For whoever are led by the Spirit of God, they are the sons of God. . . . The Spirit Himself gives testimony to our own spirit that we are the sons of God." "To as many as received Him He gave the power to become the sons of God. . . ." And so the contemplation of which I speak is a religious and transcendent gift. It is not something to which we can attain alone, by intellectual effort, by perfecting our natural powers. It is not a kind of self-hypnosis, resulting from concentration on our own inner spiritual being. It is not the fruit of our own efforts. It is the gift of God who, in His mercy, completes the hidden and mysterious work of creation in us by enlightening our minds and hearts, by awakening in us the awareness that we are words spoken in His One Word, and that Creating Spirit (*Creator Spiritus*) dwells in us, and we in Him. That we are "in Christ" and that Christ lives in us. That the natural life in us has been completed, elevated, transformed and fulfilled in Christ by the Holy Spirit. Contemplation is the awareness and realization, even in some sense *experience*, of what each Christian obscurely believes: "It is now no longer I that live but Christ lives in me."

Hence contemplation is more than a consideration of abstract truths about God, more even than affective meditation on the things we believe. It is awakening, enlightenment and the amazing intuitive grasp by which love gains certitude of God's creative and dynamic intervention in our daily life. Hence contemplation does not simply "find" a clear idea of God and confine Him within the limits of that idea, and hold Him there as a prisoner to whom it can always return. On the contrary, contemplation is carried away by Him into His own realm, His own mystery and His own freedom. It is a pure and a virginal knowledge, poor in concepts, poorer still in reasoning, but able, by its very poverty and purity, to follow the Word "wherever He may go."

2

What Contemplation is Not

THE only way to get rid of misconceptions about contemplation is to experience it. One who does not actually know, in his own life, the nature of this breakthrough and this awakening to a new level of reality cannot help being misled by most of the things that are said about it. For contemplation cannot be taught. It cannot even be clearly explained. It can only be hinted at, suggested, pointed to, symbolized. The more objectively and scientifically one tries to analyse it, the more he empties it of its real content, for this experience is beyond the reach of verbalization and of rationalization. Nothing is more repellent than a pseudo-scientific definition of the contemplative experience. One reason for this is that he who attempts such a definition is tempted to proceed psychologically, and there is really no adequate *psychology* of contemplation. To describe "reactions" and "feelings" is to situate contemplation where it is not to be found, in the superficial consciousness where it can be observed by reflection. But this reflection and this consciousness are precisely part of that external self which "dies" and is cast aside like a soiled garment in the genuine awakening of the contemplative.

Contemplation is not and cannot be a function of this external self. There is an irreducible opposition between the deep transcendent self that awakens only in contemplation, and the superficial, external self which we commonly identify with the first person singular. We must remember that this superficial "I" is not our real self. It is our "individuality" and

5

our "empirical self" but it is not truly the hidden and mysterious person in whom we subsist before the eyes of God. The "I" that works in the world, thinks about itself, observes its own reactions and talks about itself is not the true "I" that has been united to God in Christ. It is at best the vesture, the mask, the disguise of that mysterious and unknown "self" whom most of us never discover until we are dead.* Our external, superficial self is not eternal, not spiritual. Far from it. This self is doomed to disappear as completely as smoke from a chimney. It is utterly frail and evanescent. Contemplation is precisely the awareness that this "I" is really "not I" and the awakening of the unknown "I" that is beyond observation and reflection and is incapable of commenting upon itself. It cannot even say "I" with the assurance and the impertinence of the other one, for its very nature is to be hidden, unnamed, unidentified in the society where men talk about themselves and about one another. In such a world the true "I" remains both inarticulate and invisible, because it has altogether too much to say—not one word of which is about itself.

Nothing could be more alien to contemplation than the *cogito ergo sum* of Descartes. "I think, therefore I am." This is the declaration of an alienated being, in exile from his own spiritual depths, compelled to seek some comfort in a *proof for his own existence*(!) based on the observation that he "thinks." If his thought is necessary as a medium through which he arrives at the concept of his existence, then he is in fact only moving further away from his true being. He is reducing himself to a concept. He is making it impossible for himself to experience, directly and immediately, the mystery of his own being. At the same time, by also reducing God to a concept, he makes it impossible for himself to have any intuition of the divine

---

*"Hell" can be described as a perpetual alienation from our true being, our true self, which is in God.

reality which is inexpressible. He arrives at his own being as if it were an objective reality, that is to say he strives to become aware of himself as he would of some "thing" alien to himself. And he proves that the "thing" exists. He convinces himself: "I am therefore some *thing*." And then he goes on to convince himself that God, the infinite, the transcendent, is also a "thing," an "object," like other finite and limited objects of our thought!

Contemplation, on the contrary, is the experiential grasp of reality as *subjective*, not so much "mine" (which would signify "belonging to the external self") but "myself" in existential mystery. Contemplation does not arrive at reality after a process of deduction, but by an intuitive awakening in which our free and personal reality becomes fully alive to its own existential depths, which open out into the mystery of God.

For the contemplative there is no *cogito* ("I think") and no *ergo* ("therefore") but only *SUM*, I Am. Not in the sense of a futile assertion of our individuality as ultimately real, but in the humble realization of our mysterious being as persons in whom God dwells, with infinite sweetness and inalienable power.

Obviously contemplation is not just the affair of a passive and quiet temperament. It is not mere inertia, a tendency to inactivity, to psychic peace. The contemplative is not merely a man who likes to sit and think, still less one who sits around with a vacant stare. Contemplation is much more than thoughtfulness or a taste for reflection. Certainly, a thoughtful and reflective disposition is nothing to be despised in our world of inanity and automatism—and it can very well dispose a man for contemplation.

Contemplation is not prayerfulness, or a tendency to find peace and satisfaction in liturgical rites. These, too, are a great good, and they are almost necessary preparations for contemplative experience. They can never, of themselves, constitute that experience. Contemplative intuition has nothing to do with temperament. Though it sometimes happens that a man of quiet temperament becomes a contemplative, it may also happen that the very passivity of his character keeps him from suffering the inner struggle and the crisis through which one generally comes to a deeper spiritual awakening.

On the other hand, it can happen that an active and passionate man awakens to contemplation, and perhaps suddenly, without too much struggle. But it must be said, as a rule, that certain active types are not disposed to contemplation and never come to it except with great difficulty. Indeed, they ought perhaps not even to think about it or seek it, because in doing so they will tend to strain themselves and injure themselves by absurd efforts that cannot possibly make any sense or have any useful purpose. Such people, being given to imagination, passion and active conquest, exhaust themselves in trying to attain contemplation as if it were some kind of an object, like a material fortune, or a political office, or a professorship, or a prelacy. But contemplation can never be the object of calculated ambition. It is not something we plan to obtain with our practical reason, but the living water of the spirit that we thirst for, like a hunted deer thirsting after a river in the wilderness.

It is not we who choose to awaken ourselves, but God who chooses to awaken us.

Contemplation is not a trance or ecstasy, nor the hearing of sudden unutterable words, nor the imagination of lights. It is the emotional fire and sweetness that come with religious exaltation. It is not enthusiasm, the sense of being "seized" by an elemental force and swept into liberation by mystical frenzy. These things may seem to be in some way like a contemplative awakening in so far as they suspend the ordinary awareness and control exercised by our empirical self. But they are not the work of the "deep self," only of the emotions, of the somatic unconscious. They are a flooding up of the dionysian forces of the "id." Such manifestations can of course accompany a deep and genuine religious experience, but they are not what I am talking about here as contemplation.

NOR is contemplation the gift of prophecy, nor does it imply the ability to read the secrets of men's hearts. These things can sometimes go along with contemplation but they are not essential to it, and it would be erroneous to confuse them with it.

There are many other escapes from the empirical, external self which might seem to be, but are not, contemplation. For instance, the experience of being seized and taken out of oneself by collective enthusiasm, in a totalitarian parade: the self-righteous upsurge of party loyalty that blots out conscience and absolves every criminal tendency in the name of Class, Nation, Party, Race or Sect. The danger and the attraction of these false mystiques of Nation and of Class is precisely that they seduce and pretend to satisfy those who are no longer aware of any deep or genuine spiritual need. The false mysticism of the Mass Society captivates men who are so alienated from themselves and from God that they are no longer capable of genuine spiritual experience. Yet it is precisely these ersatz forms of enthusiasm that are "opium" for the people, deadening their awareness of their deepest and most personal needs, alienating them from their true selves, putting conscience and personality to sleep and turning free, reasonable men into passive instruments of the power politician.

Let no one hope to find in contemplation an escape from conflict, from anguish or from doubt. On the contrary, the deep, inexpressible certitude of the contemplative experience awakens a tragic anguish and opens many questions in the depths of the heart like wounds that cannot stop bleeding. For every gain in deep certitude there is a corresponding growth of superficial "doubt." This doubt is by no means opposed to genuine faith, but it mercilessly examines and questions the spurious "faith" of everyday life, the human faith which is nothing but the passive acceptance of conventional opinion. This false "faith" which is what we often live by and which we even come to confuse with our "religion" is subjected to inexorable questioning. This torment is a kind of trial by fire in which we are compelled, by the very light of invisible truth which has reached us in the dark ray of contemplation, to examine, to doubt and finally to reject all the prejudices and conventions that we have hitherto accepted as if they were dogmas. Hence is it clear that genuine contemplation is incompatible with complacency and with smug acceptance of prejudiced opinions. It is not mere passive acquiescence in the *status quo*, as some would like to believe—for this would reduce it to the level of spiritual anaesthesia. Contemplation is no pain-killer. What a holocaust takes place in this steady burning to ashes of old worn-out words, clichés, slogans, rationalizations! The worst of it is that even apparently *holy* conceptions are consumed along with all the rest. It is a terrible breaking and burning of idols, a purification of the sanctuary, so that no graven thing may occupy the place that God has commanded to be left empty: the centre, the existential altar which simply "is."

In the end the contemplative suffers the anguish of realizing that he *no longer knows what God is*. He may or may not mercifully realize that, after all, this is a great gain, because "God is not a *what*," not a "thing." That is precisely one of the essential characteristics of contemplative experience. It sees that there is no "what" that can be called God. There is "no such thing" as God because God is neither a "what" nor a "thing" but a pure "*Who*."* He is the "Thou" before whom our inmost "I" springs into awareness. He is the I Am before whom with our own most personal and inalienable voice we echo "I am."

*This should not be taken to mean that man has no valid concept of the divine nature. Yet in contemplation abstract notions of the divine essence no longer play an important part since they are replaced by a concrete intuition, based on love, of God as a *Person*, an object of love, not a "nature" or a "thing" which would be the object of study or of possessive desire.

3

Seeds of Contemplation

EVERY moment and every event of every man's life on earth plant something in his soul. For just as the wind carries thousands of winged seeds, so each moment brings with it germs of spiritual vitality that come to rest imperceptibly in the minds and wills of men. Most of these unnumbered seeds perish and are lost, because men are not prepared to receive them: for such seeds as these cannot spring up anywhere except in the good soil of freedom, spontaneity and love.

This is no new idea. Christ in the parable of the sower long ago told us that "The seed is the word of God." We often think this applies only to the word of the Gospel as formally preached in churches on Sundays (if indeed it is preached in churches any more!). But every expression of the will of God is in some sense a "word" of God and therefore a "seed" of new life. The ever-changing reality in the midst of which we live should awaken us to the possibility of an uninterrupted dialogue with God. By this I do not mean continuous "talk," or a frivolously conversational form of affective prayer which is sometimes cultivated in convents, but a dialogue of love and of choice. A dialogue of deep wills.

In all the situations of life the "will of God" comes to us not merely as an external dictate of impersonal law but above all as an interior invitation of personal love. Too often the conventional conception of "God's will" as a sphinx-like and arbitrary force bearing down upon us with implacable hostility, leads men to lose faith in a God they cannot find it possible to love. Such a view of the divine will drives human weakness to despair and one wonders if it is not, itself, often the expression of a despair too intolerable to be admitted to conscious consideration. These arbitrary "dictates" of a domineering and insensible Father are more often seeds of hatred than of love. If that is our concept of the will of God, we cannot possibly seek the obscure and intimate mystery of the encounter that takes place in contemplation. We will desire only to fly as far as possible from Him and hide from His face forever. So much depends on our idea of God! Yet no idea of Him, however pure and perfect, is adequate to express Him as He really is. Our idea of God tells us more about ourselves than about Him.

We must learn to realize that the love of God seeks us in every situation, and seeks our good. His inscrutable love seeks our awakening. True, since this awakening implies a kind of death to our exterior self, we will dread His coming in proportion as we are identified with this exterior self and attached to it. But when we understand the dialectic of life and death we will learn to take the risks implied by faith, to make the choices that deliver us from our routine self and open to us the door of a new being, a new reality.

The mind that is the prisoner of conventional ideas, and the will that is the captive of its own desire cannot accept the seeds of an unfamiliar truth and a supernatural desire. For how can I receive the seeds of freedom if I am in love with slavery and how can I cherish the desire of God if I am filled with another and an opposite desire? God cannot plant His liberty in me because I am a prisoner and I do not even desire to be free. I love my captivity and I imprison myself in the desire for the things that I hate, and I have hardened my heart against true love. I must learn therefore to let go of the familiar and the usual and consent to what is new and unknown to me. I must learn to "leave myself" in order to find myself by yielding to the love of God. If I were looking for God, every event and every moment would sow, in my will, grains of His life that would spring up one day in a tremendous harvest.

For it is God's love that warms me in the sun and God's love that sends the cold rain. It is God's love that feeds me in the bread I eat and God that feeds me also by hunger and fasting. It is the love of God that sends the winter days when I am cold and sick, and the hot summer when I labour and my clothes are full of sweat: but it is God who breathes on me with light winds off the river and in the breezes out of the wood. His love spreads the shade of the sycamore over my head and sends the water-boy along the edge of the wheat field with a bucket from the spring, while the labourers are resting and the mules stand under the tree.

It is God's love that speaks to me in the birds and streams; but also behind the clamour of the city God speaks to me in His judgements, and all these things are seeds sent to me from His will.

If these seeds would take root in my liberty, and if His will would grow from my freedom, I would become the love that He is, and my harvest would be His glory and my own joy.

And I would grow together with thousands and millions of other freedoms into the gold of one huge field praising God, loaded with increase, loaded with wheat. If in all things I consider only the heat and the cold, the food or the hunger, the sickness or labour, the beauty or pleasure, the success and failure or the material good or evil my works have won for my own will, I will find only emptiness and not happiness. I shall not be fed, I shall not be full. For my food is the will of Him who made me and who made all things in order to give Himself to me through them.

My chief care should not to be find pleasure or success, health or life or money or rest or even things like virtue and wisdom—still less their opposites, pain, failure, sickness, death. But in all that happens, my one desire and my one joy should be to know: "Here is the thing that God has willed for me. In this His love is found, and in accepting this I can give back His love to Him and give myself with it to Him. For in giving myself I shall find Him and He is life everlasting."

By consenting to His will with joy and doing it with gladness I have His love in my heart, because my will is now the same as His love and I am on the way to becoming what He is, who is Love. And by accepting all things from Him I receive His joy into my soul, not because things are what they are but because God is who He is, and His love has willed my joy in them all.

How am I to know the will of God? Even where there is no other more explicit claim on my obedience, such as a legitimate command, the very nature of each situation usually bears written into itself some indication of God's will. For whatever is demanded by truth, by justice, by mercy, or by love must surely be taken to be willed by God. To consent to His will is, then, to consent to be true, or to speak truth, or at least to seek it. To obey Him is to respond to His will expressed in the need of another person, or at least to respect the rights of others. For the right of another man is the expression of God's love and God's will. In demanding that I respect the rights of another God is not merely asking me to conform to some abstract, arbitrary law: He is enabling me to share, as His son, in His own care for my brother. No man who ignores the rights and needs of others can hope to walk in the light of contemplation, because his way has turned aside from truth, from compassion and therefore from God.

The requirements of a work to be done can be understood as the will of God. If I am supposed to hoe a garden or make a table, then I will be obeying God if I am true to the task I am performing. To do the work carefully and well, with love and respect for the nature of my task and with due attention to its purpose, is to unite myself to God's will in my work. In this way I become His instrument. He works through me. When I act as His instrument my labour cannot become an obstacle to contemplation, even though it may temporarily so occupy my mind that I cannot engage in it while I am actually doing my job. Yet my work itself will purify and pacify my mind and dispose me for contemplation.

Unnatural, frantic, anxious work, work done under pressure of greed or fear or any other inordinate passion, cannot properly speaking be dedicated to God, because God never wills such work directly. He may permit that through no fault of our own we may have to work madly and distractedly, due to our sins, and to the sins of the society in which we live. In that case we must tolerate it and make the best of what we cannot avoid. But let us not be blind to the distinction between sound, healthy work and unnatural toil.

In any case, we should always seek to conform to the *logos* or truth of the duty before us, the work to be done, or our own God-given nature. Contemplative obedience and abandonment to the will of God can never mean a cultivated indifference to the natural values implanted by Him in human life and work. Insensitivity must not be confused with detachment. The contemplative must certainly be detached, but he can never allow himself to become insensible to true human values, whether in society, in other men or in himself. If he does so, then his contemplation stands condemned as vitiated in its very root.

4

Everything that is, is Holy

DETACHMENT from things does not mean setting up a contradiction between "things" and "God" as if God were another "thing" and as if His creatures were His rivals. We do not detach ourselves from things in order to attach ourselves to God, but rather we become detached *from ourselves* in order to see and use all things in and for God. This is an entirely new perspective which many sincerely moral and ascetic minds fail utterly to see. There is no evil in anything created by God, nor can anything of His become an obstacle to our union with Him. The obstacle is in our "self," that is to say in the tenacious need to maintain our separate, external, egotistic will. It is when we refer all things to this outward and false "self" that we alienate ourselves from reality and from God. It is then the false self that is our god, and we love everything for the sake of this self. We use all things, so to speak, for the worship of this idol which is our imaginary self. In so doing we pervert and corrupt things, or rather we turn our relationship to them into a corrupt and sinful relationship. We do not thereby make them evil, but we use them to increase our attachment to our illusory self.

Those who try to escape from this situation by treating the good things of God as if they were evils are only confirming themselves in a terrible illusion. They are like Adam blaming Eve and Eve blaming the serpent in Eden. "Woman has tempted me. Wine has tempted me. Food has tempted me. Woman is pernicious, wine is poison, food is death. I must hate and revile them. By hating them I will please God. . . ." These are the thoughts and attitudes of a baby, of a savage and of an idolater who seeks by magic incantations and spells to protect his egotistic self and placate the insatiable little god in his own heart. To take such an idol for God is the worst kind of self-deception. It turns a man into a fanatic, no longer capable of sustained contact with the truth, no longer capable of genuine love.

In trying to believe in their ego as something "holy" these fanatics look upon everything else as unholy.

It is not true that the saints and the great contemplatives never loved created things, and had no understanding or appreciation of the world, with its sights and sounds and the people living in it. They loved everything and everyone.

Do you think that their love of God was compatible with a hatred for things that reflected Him and spoke of Him on every side?

You will say that they were supposed to be absorbed in God and they had no eyes to see anything but Him. Do you think they walked around with faces like stones and did not listen to the voices of men speaking to them or understand the joys and sorrows of those who were around them?

It was because the saints were absorbed in God that they were truly capable of seeing and appreciating created things and it was because they loved Him alone that they alone loved everybody.

Some men seem to think that a saint cannot possibly take a natural interest in anything created. They imagine that any form of spontaneity or enjoyment is a sinful gratification of "fallen nature." That to be "supernatural" means obstructing all spontaneity with clichés and arbitrary references to God.

The purpose of these clichés is, so to speak, to hold everything at arm's length, to frustrate spontaneous reactions, to exorcise feelings of guilt. Or perhaps to cultivate such feelings! One wonders sometimes if such morality is not after all a love of guilt! They suppose that the life of a saint can never be anything but a perpetual duel with guilt, and that a saint cannot even drink a glass of cold water without making an act of contrition for slaking his thirst, as if that were a mortal sin. As if for the saints every response to beauty, to goodness, to the pleasant, were an offence. As if the saint could never allow himself to be pleased with anything but his prayers and his interior acts of piety.

A saint is capable of loving created things and enjoying the use of them and dealing with them in a perfectly simple, natural manner, making no formal references to God, drawing no attention to his own piety, and acting without any artificial rigidity at all. His gentleness and his sweetness are not pressed through his pores by the crushing restraint of a spiritual strait-jacket. They come from his direct docility to the light of truth and to the will of God. Hence a saint is capable of talking about the world without any explicit reference to God, in such a way that his statement gives greater glory to God and arouses a greater love of God than the observations of someone less holy, who has to strain himself to make an arbitrary connection between creatures and God through the medium of hackneyed analogies and metaphors that are so feeble that they make you think there is something the matter with religion.

The saint knows that the world and everything made by God is good, while those who are not saints either think that created things are unholy, or else they don't bother about the question one way or another because they are only interested in themselves.

The eyes of the saint make all beauty holy and the hands of the saint consecrate everything they touch to the glory of God, and the saint is never offended by anything and judges no man's sin because he does not know sin. He knows the mercy of God. He knows that his own mission on earth is to bring that mercy to all men.

WHEN we are one with God's love, we own all things in Him. They are ours to offer Him in Christ His Son. For all things belong to the sons of God and we are Christ's and Christ is God's. Resting in His glory above all pleasure and pain, joy or sorrow, and every other good or evil, we love in all things His will rather than the things themselves, and that is the way we make creation a sacrifice in praise of God.

This is the end for which all things were made by God.

THE only true joy on earth is to escape from the prison of our own false self, and enter by love into union with the Life who dwells and sings within the essence of every creature and in the core of our own souls. In His love we possess all things and enjoy fruition of them, finding Him in them all. And thus as we go about the world, everything we meet and everything we see and hear and touch, far from defiling, purifies us and plants in us something more of contemplation and of heaven.

Short of this perfection, created things do not bring us joy but pain. Until we love God perfectly, everything in the world will be able to hurt us. And the greatest misfortune is to be dead to the pain they inflict on us, and not to realize what it is.

For until we love God perfectly His world is full of contradictions. The things He has created attract us to Him and yet keep us away from Him. They draw us on and they stop us

dead. We find Him in them to some extent and then we don't
find Him in them at all.

Just when we think we have discovered some joy in them,
the joy turns into sorrow; and just when they are beginning to
please us the pleasure turns into pain.

In all created things we, who do not yet perfectly love God,
can find something that reflects the fulfilment of heaven and
something that reflects the anguish of hell. We find something
of the joy of blessedness and something of the pain of loss,
which is damnation.

The fulfilment we find in creatures belongs to the reality of
the created being, a reality that is from God and belongs to
God and reflects God. The anguish we find in them belongs to
the disorder of our desire which looks for a greater reality in
the object of our desire than is actually there: a greater fulfilment than any created thing is capable of giving. Instead of
worshipping God through His creation we are always trying
to worship ourselves by means of creatures.

But to worship our false selves is to worship nothing. And
the worship of nothing is hell.

THE "false self" must not be identified with the body. The
body is neither evil nor unreal. It has a reality that is given it by
God, and this reality is therefore holy. Hence we say rightly,
though symbolically, that the body is the "temple of God,"
meaning that His truth, His perfect reality, is enshrined there
in the mystery of our own being. Let no one, then, dare to
hate or to despise the body that has been entrusted to him by
God, and let no one dare to misuse this body. Let him not
desecrate his own natural unity by dividing himself, soul against
body, as if the soul were good and the body evil. Soul and
body together subsist in the reality of the hidden, inner person.
If the two are separated from one another, there is no longer a

person, there is no longer a living, subsisting reality made in the image and likeness of God. The "marriage" of body and soul in one person is one of the things that makes man the image of God; and what God has joined no man can separate without danger to his sanity.

It is equally false to treat the soul as if it were the "whole self" and the body as if it were the "whole self." Those who make the first mistake fall into the sin of angelism. Those who make the second live below the level assigned by God to human nature. (It would be an easy cliché to say they live like beasts: but this is not always true, by any means.) There are many respectable and even conventionally moral people for whom there is no other reality in life than their body and its relationship with "things." They have reduced themselves to a life lived within the limits of their five senses. Their self is consequently an illusion based on sense experience and nothing else. For these the body becomes a source of falsity and deception: but that is not the body's fault. It is the fault of the person himself, who consents to the illusion, who finds security in self-deception and will not answer the secret voice of God calling him to take a risk and venture by faith outside the reassuring and protective limits of his five senses.

5

Things in their Identity

A TREE gives glory to God by being a tree. For in being what God means it to be it is obeying Him. It "consents," so to speak, to His creative love. It is expressing an idea which is in God and which is not distinct from the essence of God, and therefore a tree imitates God by being a tree.

The more a tree is like itself, the more it is like Him. If it tried to be like something else which it was never intended to be, it would be less like God and therefore it would give Him less glory.

No two created beings are exactly alike. And their individuality is no imperfection. On the contrary, the perfection of each created thing is not merely in its conformity to an abstract type but in its own individual identity with itself. This particular tree will give glory to God by spreading out its roots in the earth and raising its branches into the air and the light in a way that no other tree before or after it ever did or will do.

Do you imagine that the individual created things in the world are imperfect attempts at reproducing an ideal type which the Creator never quite succeeded in actualizing on earth? If that is so they do not give Him glory but proclaim that He is not a perfect Creator.

Therefore each particular being, in its individuality, its concrete nature and entity, with all its own characteristics and its private qualities and its own inviolable identity, gives glory to God by being precisely what He wants it to be here and

now, in the circumstances ordained for it by His Love and
His infinite Art.

THE forms and individual characters of living and growing
things, of inanimate beings, of animals and flowers and all
nature, constitute their holiness in the sight of God.

Their inscape is their sanctity. It is the imprint of His
wisdom and His reality in them.

The special clumsy beauty of this particular colt on this
April day in this field under these clouds is a holiness consecrated to God by His own creative wisdom and it declares the
glory of God.

The pale flowers of the dogwood outside this window are
saints. The little yellow flowers that nobody notices on the
edge of that road are saints looking up into the face of God.

This leaf has its own texture and its own pattern of veins
and its own holy shape, and the bass and trout hiding in the
deep pools of the river are canonized by their beauty and their
strength.

The lakes hidden among the hills are saints, and the sea too
is a saint who praises God without interruption in her majestic
dance.

The great, gashed, half-naked mountain is another of God's
saints. There is no other like him. He is alone in his own
character; nothing else in the world ever did or ever will
imitate God in quite the same way. That is his sanctity.

BUT what about you? What about me?

Unlike the animals and the trees, it is not enough for us to
be what our nature intends. It is not enough for us to be individual men. For us, holiness is more than humanity. If we are
never anything but men, never anything but people, we will

not be saints and we will not be able to offer to God the worship of our imitation, which is sanctity.

It is true to say that for me sanctity consists in being myself and for you sanctity consists in being *your* self and that, in the last analysis, your sanctity will never be mine and mine will never be yours, except in the communism of charity and grace.

FOR me to be a saint means to be myself. Therefore the problem of sanctity and salvation is in fact the problem of finding out who I am and of discovering my true self.

Trees and animals have no problem. God makes them what they are without consulting them, and they are perfectly satisfied.

With us it is different. God leaves us free to be whatever we like. We can be ourselves or not, as we please. We are at liberty to be real, or to be unreal. We may be true or false, the choice is ours. We may wear now one mask and now another, and never, if we so desire, appear with our own true face. But we cannot make these choices with impunity. Causes have effects, and if we lie to ourselves and to others, then we cannot expect to find truth and reality whenever we happen to want them. If we have chosen the way of falsity we must not be surprised that truth eludes us when we finally come to need it!

OUR vocation is not simply to *be*, but to work together with God in the creation of our own life, our own identity, our own destiny. We are free beings and sons of God. This means to say that we should not passively exist, but actively participate in His creative freedom, in our own lives, and in the lives of others, by choosing the truth. To put it better, we are even called to share with God the work of *creating* the truth of our identity. We can evade this responsibility by playing with masks, and this pleases us because it can appear at times to be a free and creative way of living. It is quite easy, it seems to please everyone. But in the long run the cost and the sorrow come very high. To work out our own identity in God, which the Bible calls "working out our salvation," is a labour that requires sacrifice and anguish, risk and many tears. It demands close attention to reality at every moment, and great fidelity to God as He reveals Himself, obscurely, in the mystery of each new situation. We do not know clearly beforehand what the result of this work will be. The secret of my full identity is hidden in Him. He alone can make me who I am, or rather who I will be when at last I fully begin to be. But unless I desire this identity and work to find it with Him and in Him, the work will never be done. The way of doing it is a secret I can learn from no one else but Him. There is no way of attaining to the secret without faith. But contemplation is the greater and more precious gift, for it enables me to see and understand the work that He wants done.

The seeds that are planted in my liberty at every moment, by God's will, are the seeds of my own identity, my own reality, my own happiness, my own sanctity.

To refuse them is to refuse everything; it is the refusal of my own existence and being: of my identity, my very self.

Not to accept and love and do God's will is to refuse the fullness of my existence.

If I never become what I am meant to be, but always remain what I am not, I shall spend eternity contradicting myself by being at once something and nothing, a life that wants to live and is dead, a death that wants to be dead and cannot quite achieve its own death because it still has to exist.

To say I was born in sin is to say I came into the world with a false self. I was born in a mask. I came into existence under a sign of contradiction, being someone that I was never intended to be and therefore a denial of what I am supposed to be. And thus I came into existence and nonexistence at the same time because from the very start I was something that I was not.

To say the same thing without paradox: as long as I am no longer anybody else than the thing that was born of my mother, I am so far short of being the person I ought to be that I might as well not exist at all. In fact, it were better for me that I had not been born.

EVERY one of us is shadowed by an illusory person: a false self.

This is the man that I want myself to be but who cannot exist, because God does not know anything about him. And to be unknown of God is altogether too much privacy.

My false and private self is the one who wants to exist outside the reach of God's will and God's love—outside of reality and outside of life. And such a self cannot help but be an illusion.

We are not very good at recognizing illusions, least of all the ones we cherish about ourselves—the ones we are born with and which feed the roots of sin. For most of the people in the world, there is no greater subjective reality than this false self of theirs, which cannot exist. A life devoted to the cult of this shadow is what is called a life of sin.

All sin starts from the assumption that my false self, the self that exists only in my own egocentric desires, is the fundamental reality of life to which everything else in the universe is ordered. Thus I use up my life in the desire for pleasures and the thirst for experiences, for power, honour, knowledge and love, to clothe this false self and construct its nothingness into something objectively real. And I wind experiences around myself and cover myself with pleasures and glory like bandages in order to make myself perceptible to myself and to the world, as if I were an invisible body that could only become visible when something visible covered its surface.

But there is no substance under the things with which I am clothed. I am hollow, and my structure of pleasures and ambitions has no foundation. I am objectified in them. But they are all destined by their very contingency to be destroyed. And when they are gone there will be nothing left of me but my own nakedness and emptiness and hollowness, to tell me that I am my own mistake.

THE secret of my identity is hidden in the love and mercy of God.

But whatever is in God is really identical with Him, for His infinite simplicity admits no division and no distinction. Therefore I cannot hope to find myself anywhere except in Him.

Ultimately the only way that I can be myself is to become identified with Him in whom is hidden the reason and fulfilment of my existence.

Therefore there is only one problem on which all my existence, my peace and my happiness depend: to discover myself in discovering God. If I find Him I will find myself and if I find my true self I will find Him.

But although this looks simple, it is in reality immensely difficult. In fact, if I am left to myself it will be utterly impossible. For although I can know something of God's existence and nature by my own reason, there is no human and rational way in which I can arrive at that contact, that possession of Him, which will be the discovery of who He really is and of who I am in Him.

That is something that no man can ever do alone.

Nor can all the men and all the created things in the universe help him in this work.

The only One who can teach me to find God is God, Himself, Alone.

6

Pray for your own Discovery

THERE exists some point at which I can meet God in a real and experimental contact with His infinite actuality. This is the "place" of God, His sanctuary—it is the point where my contingent being depends upon His love. Within myself is a metaphorical apex of existence at which I am held in being by my Creator.

God utters me like a word containing a partial thought of Himself.

A word will never be able to comprehend the voice that utters it.

But if I am true to the concept that God utters in me, if I am true to the thought of Him I was meant to embody, I shall be full of His actuality and find Him everywhere in myself, and find myself nowhere. I shall be lost in Him: that is, I shall find myself. I shall be "saved."

It is a pity that the beautiful Christian metaphor "salvation" has come to be so hackneyed and therefore so despised. It has been turned into a vapid synonym for "piety"—not even a truly ethical concept. "Salvation" is something far beyond ethical propriety. The word connotes a deep respect for the fundamental metaphysical reality of man. It reflects God's own infinite concern for man, God's love and care for man's inmost being, God's love for all that is His own in man, His son. It is not only human nature that is "saved" by the divine mercy, but above all the human *person*. The object of salvation is that which is unique, irreplaceable, incommunicable—that which is myself alone. This true inner self must be drawn up like a jewel from the bottom of the sea, rescued from confusion, from indistinction, from immersion in the common, the nondescript, the trivial, the sordid, the evanescent.

We must be saved from immersion in the sea of lies and passions which is called "the world." And we must be saved above all from that abyss of confusion and absurdity which is our own worldly self. The person must be rescued from the individual. The free son of God must be saved from the conformist slave of fantasy, passion and convention. The creative and mysterious inner self must be delivered from the wasteful, hedonistic and destructive ego that seeks only to cover itself with disguises.

To be "lost" is to be left to the arbitrariness and pretences of the contingent ego, the smoke-self that must inevitably vanish. To be "saved" is to return to one's inviolate and eternal reality and to live in God.

WHAT one of you can enter into himself and find the God who utters him?

"Finding God" means much more than just abandoning all things that are not God, and emptying oneself of images and desires.

If you succeed in emptying your mind of every thought and every desire, you may indeed withdraw into the centre of yourself and concentrate everything within you upon the imaginary point where your life springs out of God: yet you will not really find God. No natural exercise can bring you into vital contact with Him. Unless He utters Himself in you, speaks His own name in the centre of your soul, you will no more know Him than a stone knows the ground upon which it rests in its inertia.

OUR discovery of God is, in a way, God's discovery of us. We cannot go to heaven to find Him because we have no way of knowing where heaven is or what it is. He comes down from heaven and finds us. He looks at us from the depths of His own infinite actuality, which is everywhere, and His seeing us gives us a new being and a new mind in which we also discover Him. We only know Him in so far as we are known by Him, and our contemplation of Him is a participation in His contemplation of Himself.

We become contemplatives when God discovers Himself in us.

At that moment the point of our contact with Him opens out and we pass through the centre of our own nothingness and enter into infinite reality, where we awaken as our true self.

It is true that God knows Himself in all the things that exist. He sees them, and it is because He sees them that they exist. It is because He loves them that they are good. His love in them is their intrinsic goodness. The value He sees in them is their value. In so far as He sees and loves them, all things reflect Him.

But although God is present in all things by His knowledge and His love and His power and His care of them, He is not necessarily realized and known by them. He is only known and loved by those to whom He has freely given a share in His own knowledge and love of Himself.

In order to know and love God as He is, we must have God dwelling in us in a new way, not only in His creative power but in His mercy, not only in His greatness but in His littleness, by which He empties Himself and comes down to us to be empty in our emptiness, and so fill us in His fullness. God bridges the infinite distances between Himself and the spirits created to love Him, by supernatural missions of His own life. The Father, dwelling in the depths of all things and

in my own depths, communicates to me His Word and His
Spirit. Receiving them I am drawn into His own life and
know God in His own Love, being one with Him in His own
Son.

My discovery of my identity begins and is perfected in these
missions, because it is in them that God Himself, bearing in
Himself the secret of who I am, begins to live in me not only
as my Creator but as my other and true self. *Vivo, iam non ego,
vivit vero in me Christus* ("I live, now not I, but Christ lives in
me").

THESE missions begin at Baptism. But they do not take on any
practical meaning in the life of our spirit until we become
capable of conscious acts of love. From then on God's special
presence in us corresponds to our own free decisions. From
then on our life becomes a series of choices between the fiction
of our false self, whom we feed with the illusions of passion
and selfish appetite, and our loving consent to the purely
gratuitous mercy of God.

When I consent to the will and the mercy of God as it
"comes" to me in the events of life, appealing to my inner self
and awakening my faith, I break through the superficial
exterior appearances that form my routine vision of the world
and of my own self, and I find myself in the presence of hidden
majesty. It may appear to me that this majesty and presence is
something objective, "outside myself." Indeed, the primitive
saints and prophets *saw* this divine presence in vision as a light
or an angel or a man or a burning fire, or a blazing glory
upheld by cherubim. Only thus could their minds do justice
to the supreme reality of what they experienced. Yet this is a
majesty we do not *see* with our eyes and it is all within ourselves. It is the mission of the Word and the Spirit, from the
Father, in the depths of our own being. It is a majesty com-

municate to us, shared with us, so that our whole being is filled with the gift of glory and responds with adoration.

This is the "mercy of God" revealed to us by the secret missions in which He gives Himself to us, and awakens our identity as sons and heirs of His Kingdom. This is the Kingdom of God within us, and for the coming of this Kingdom we pray each time we say the "Our Father." In the revelation of mercy and majesty we come to an obscure intuition of our own personal secret, our true identity. Our inner self awakens, with a momentary flash, in the instant of recognition when we say "Yes!" to the indwelling Divine Persons. We are only really ourselves when we completely consent to "receive" the glory of God into ourselves. Our true self is, then, the self that receives freely and gladly the missions that are God's supreme gift to His sons. Any other "self" is only an illusion.

As long as I am on earth my mind and will remain more or less impervious to the missions of God's Word and His Spirit. I do not easily receive His light.

Every movement of my own natural appetite, even though my nature is good in itself, tends in one way or another to keep alive in me the illusion that is opposed to God's reality living within me. Even though my natural acts are good they have a tendency, when they are only natural, to concentrate my faculties on the man that I am not, the one I cannot be, the false self in me, the character that God does not know. This is because I am born in selfishness. I am born self-centred. And this is original sin.

Even when I try to please God, I tend to please my own ambition, His enemy. There can be imperfection even in the ardent love of great perfection, even in the desire of virtue, of sanctity. Even the desire of contemplation can be impure, when we forget that true contemplation means the complete destruction of all selfishness—the most pure poverty and cleanness of heart.

ALTHOUGH God lives in the souls of men who are unconscious of Him, how can I say that I have found Him and found myself in Him if I never know Him or think of Him, never take any interest in Him or seek Him or desire His presence in my soul? What good does it do to say a few formal prayers to Him and then turn away and give all my mind and all my will to created things, desiring only ends that fall far short of Him? Even though my soul may be justified, yet if my mind does not belong to Him then I do not belong to Him either. If my love does not reach out towards Him but scatters itself in His creation, it is because I have reduced His life in me to the level of a formality, forbidding it to move me with a truly vital influence.

Justify my soul, O God, but also from Your fountains fill my will with fire. Shine in my mind, although perhaps this means "be darkness to my experience," but occupy my heart with Your tremendous Life. Let my eyes see nothing in the world but Your glory, and let my hands touch nothing that is not for Your service. Let my tongue taste no bread that does not strengthen me to praise Your great mercy. I will hear Your voice and I will hear all harmonies You have created, singing Your hymns. Sheep's wool and cotton from the field shall warm me enough that I may live in Your service; I will give the rest to Your poor. Let me use all things for one sole reason: to find my joy in giving You glory.

Therefore keep me, above all things, from sin. Keep me from the death of deadly sin which puts hell in my soul. Keep me from the murder of lust that blinds and poisons my heart. Keep me from the sins that eat a man's flesh with irresistible fire until he is devoured. Keep me from loving money in which is hatred, from avarice and ambition that suffocate my life. Keep me from the dead works of vanity and the thankless labour in which artists destroy themselves for pride and money and reputation, and saints are smothered under the avalanche of their own importunate zeal. Stanch in me the rank wound of covetousness and the hungers that exhaust my nature with their bleeding. Stamp out the serpent envy that stings love with poison and kills all joy.

Untie my hands and deliver my heart from sloth. Set me free from the laziness that goes about disguised as activity when activity is not required of me, and from the cowardice that does what is not demanded, in order to escape sacrifice.

But give me the strength that waits upon You in silence and peace. Give me humility in which alone is rest, and deliver me from pride which is the heaviest of burdens. And possess my whole heart and soul with the simplicity of love. Occupy my whole life with the one thought and the one desire of love that I may love, not for the sake of merit, not for the sake of perfection, not for the sake of virtue, not for the sake of sanctity, but for You alone.

For there is only one thing that can satisfy love and reward it, and that is You alone.

This then is what it means to seek God perfectly: to withdraw from illusion and pleasure, from worldly anxieties and desires, from the works that God does not want, from a glory that is only human display; to keep my mind free from confusion in order that my liberty may be always at the disposal of His will; to entertain silence in my heart and listen for the voice of God; to cultivate an intellectual freedom from the images of created things in order to receive the secret contact of God in obscure love; to love all men as myself; to rest in humility and to find peace in withdrawal from conflict and competition with other men; to turn aside from controversy and put away heavy loads of judgement and censorship and criticism and the whole burden of opinions that I have no obligation to carry; to have a will that is always ready to fold back within itself and draw all the powers of the soul down from its deepest centre to rest in silent expectancy for the coming of God, poised in tranquil and effortless concentration upon the point of my dependence on Him; to gather all that I am, and have all that I can possibly suffer or do or be, and abandon them all to God in the resignation of a perfect love and blind faith and pure trust in God, to do His will.

And then to wait in peace and emptiness and oblivion of all things.

Bonum est praestolari cum silentio salutare Dei. ("It is good to wait in silence for the salvation of God.")

7

Union and Division

IN order to become myself I must cease to be what I always thought I wanted to be, and in order to find myself I must go out of myself, and in order to live I have to die.

The reason for this is that I am born in selfishness and therefore my natural efforts to make myself more real and more myself, make me less real and less myself, because they revolve around a lie.

PEOPLE who know nothing of God, and whose lives are centred on themselves, imagine that they can only find themselves by asserting their own desires and ambitions and appetites in a struggle with the rest of the world. They try to become real by imposing themselves on other people, by appropriating for themselves some share of the limited supply of created goods and thus emphasizing the difference between themselves and the other men who have less than they, or nothing at all.

They can only conceive one way of becoming real: cutting themselves off from other people and building a barrier of contrast and distinction between themselves and other men. They do not know that reality is to be sought not in division but in unity, for we are "members one of another."

The man who lives in division is not a person but only an "individual."

I have what you have not. I am what you are not. I have taken what you have failed to take and I have seized what you could never get. Therefore you suffer and I am happy, you are

37

despised and I am praised, you die and I live; you are nothing
and I am something, and I am all the more something because
you are nothing. And thus I spend my life admiring the
distance between you and me; at times this even helps me to
forget the other men who have what I have not and who have
taken what I was too slow to take and who have seized what
was beyond my reach, who are praised as I cannot be praised
and who live on my death. . . .

The man who lives in division is living in death. He cannot
find himself because he is lost; he has ceased to be a reality.
The person he believes himself to be is a bad dream. And when
he dies he will discover that he long ago ceased to exist because
God, who is infinite reality and in whose sight is the being of
everything that is, will say to him: "I know you not."

AND now I am thinking of the disease which is spiritual pride.
I am thinking of the peculiar unreality that gets into the hearts
of the saints and eats their sanctity away before it is mature.
There is something of this worm in the hearts of all religious
men. As soon as they have done something which they know
to be good in the eyes of God, they tend to take its reality to
themselves and to make it their own. They tend to destroy
their virtues by claiming them for themselves and clothing
their own private illusion of themselves with values that belong
to God. Who can escape the secret desire to breathe a different
atmosphere from the rest of men? Who can do good things
without seeking to taste in them some sweet distinction from
the common run of sinners in this world?

This sickness is most dangerous when it succeeds in looking
like humility. When a proud man thinks he is humble his case
is hopeless.

Here is a man who has done many things that were hard for
his flesh to accept. He has come through difficult trials and

done a lot of work, and by God's grace he has come to possess a habit of fortitude and self-sacrifice in which, at last, labour and suffering become easy. It is reasonable that his conscience should be at peace. But before he realizes it, the clean peace of a will united to God becomes the complacency of a will that loves its own excellence.

The pleasure that is in his heart when he does difficult things and succeeds in doing them well, tells him secretly: "I am a saint." At the same time, others seem to recognize him as different from themselves. They admire him, or perhaps avoid him—a sweet homage of sinners! The pleasure burns into a devouring fire. The warmth of that fire feels very much like the love of God. It is fed by the same virtues that nourished the flame of charity. He burns with self-admiration and thinks: "It is the fire of the love of God."

He thinks his own pride is the Holy Ghost.

The sweet warmth of pleasure becomes the criterion of all his works. The relish he savours in acts that make him admirable in his own eyes drives him to fast, or to pray, or to hide in solitude, or to write many books, or to build churches and hospitals, or to start a thousand organizations. And when he gets what he wants he thinks his sense of satisfaction is the unction of the Holy Spirit.

And the secret voice of pleasure sings in his heart: "*Non sum sicut caeteri homines*" (I am not like other men).

Once he has started on this path there is no limit to the evil his self-satisfaction may drive him to do in the name of God and of His love, and for His glory. He is so pleased with himself that he can no longer tolerate the advice of another—or the commands of a superior. When someone opposes his desires he folds his hands humbly and seems to accept it for the time being, but in his heart he is saying: "I am persecuted by worldly men. They are incapable of understanding one who is led by the Spirit of God. With the saints it has always been so."

Having become a martyr he is ten times as stubborn as before.

It is a terrible thing when such a one gets the idea he is a prophet or a messenger of God or a man with a mission to reform the world. . . . He is capable of destroying religion and making the name of God odious to men.

I MUST look for my identity, somehow, not only in God but in other men.

I will never be able to find myself if I isolate myself from the rest of mankind as if I were a different kind of being.

8

Solitude is not Separation

SOME men have perhaps become hermits with the thought that sanctity could only be attained by escape from other men. But the only justification for a life of deliberate solitude is the conviction that it will help you to love not only God but also other men. If you go into the desert merely to get away from people you dislike, you will find neither peace nor solitude; you will only isolate yourself with a tribe of devils.

Man seeks unity because he is the image of the One God. Unity implies solitude, and hence the need to be physically alone. But unity and solitude are not metaphysical isolation. He who isolates himself in order to enjoy a kind of independence in his egotistic and external self does not find unity at all, for he disintegrates into a multiplicity of conflicting passions and finally ends in confusion and total unreality. Solitude is not and can never be a narcissistic dialogue of the ego with itself. Such self-contemplation is a futile attempt to establish the finite self as infinite, to make it permanently independent of all other beings. And this is madness. Note, however, that it is not a madness peculiar to solitaries—it is much more common to those who try to assert their own unique excellence by dominating others. This is the more usual sin.

The need for true solitude is a complex and dangerous thing, but it is a real need. It is all the more real today when the collectivity tends more and more to swallow up the person in its shapeless and faceless mass. The temptation of our day is to equate "love" and "conformity"—passive subservience to the mass-mind or to the organization. This temptation is only strengthened by futile rebellion on the part of eccentrics who want to be madly and notably different and who thereby create for themselves only a new kind of dullness—a dullness that is erratic instead of predictable.

True solitude is the home of the person, false solitude the refuge of the individualist. The person is constituted by a uniquely subsisting capacity to love—by a radical ability to care for all beings made by God and loved by Him. Such a capacity is destroyed by the loss of perspective. Without a certain element of solitude there can be no compassion because when a man is lost in the wheels of a social machine he is no longer aware of human needs as a matter of personal responsibility. One can escape from men by plunging into the midst of a crowd!

Go into the desert not to escape other men but in order to find them in God.

Physical solitude has its dangers, but we must not exaggerate them. The great temptation of modern man is not physical solitude but immersion in the mass of other men, not escape to the mountains or the desert (would that more men were so tempted!) but escape into the great formless sea of irresponsibility which is the crowd. There is actually no more dangerous solitude than that of the man who is lost in a crowd, who does not know he is alone and who does not function as a person in a community either. He does not face the risks of true solitude or its responsibilities, and at the same time the multitude has taken all other responsibilities off his shoulders. Yet he is by no means free of care; he is burdened by the diffuse, anonymous anxiety, the nameless fears, the petty itching lusts and the all-pervading hostilities which fill mass society the way water fills the ocean.

Mere living in the midst of other men does not guarantee that we live in communion with them or even in communication with them. Who has less to communicate than the massman? Very often it is the solitary who has the most to say; not that he uses many words, but what he says is new, substantial, unique. It is his own. Even though he says very little, he has something to communicate, something personal which he is able to share with others. He has something real to give because he himself is real.

Where men live huddled together without true communication, there seems to be greater sharing, and a more genuine communion. But this is not communion, only immersion in the general meaninglessness of countless slogans and clichés repeated over and over again so that in the end one listens without hearing and responds without thinking. The constant din of empty words and machine noises, the endless booming of loudspeakers end by making true communication and true communion almost impossible. Each individual in the mass is insulated by thick layers of insensibility. He doesn't care, he doesn't hear, he doesn't think. He does not act, he is pushed. He does not talk, he produces conventional sounds when stimulated by the appropriate noises. He does not think, he secretes clichés.

Mere living alone does not isolate a man, mere living together does not bring men into communion. The common life can either make one more of a person or less of a person, depending whether it is truly common life or merely life in a crowd. To live in communion, in genuine dialogue with others is absolutely necessary if man is to remain human. But to live in the midst of others, sharing nothing with them but the common noise and the general distraction, isolates a man in the worst way, separates him from reality in a way that is almost painless. It divides him off and separates him from other men and from his true self. Here the sin is not in the conviction that one is not like other men, but in the belief that being like them is sufficient to cover every other sin. The complacency of the individual who admires his own excellence is bad enough, but it is more respectable than the complacency of the man who has no self-esteem because he has not even a superficial self which he can esteem. He is not a person, not an individual, only an atom. This atomized existence is sometimes praised as humility or as self-sacrifice, sometimes it is called obedience, sometimes it is devotion to the dialectic of class war. It produces a kind of peace which is not peace, but only the escape from an immediately urgent sense of conflict. It is the peace not of love but of anaesthesia. It is the peace not of self-realization and self-dedication, but of flight into irresponsibility.

THERE is no true solitude except interior solitude. And interior solitude is not possible for anyone who does not accept his right place in relation to other men. There is no true peace possible for the man who still imagines that some accident of talent or grace or virtue segregates him from other men and places him above them. Solitude is not separation.

God does not give us graces or talents or virtues for ourselves alone. We are members one of another and everything that is given to one member is given for the whole body. I do not wash my feet to make them more beautiful than my face.

The saints love their sanctity not because it separates them from the rest of us and places them above us, but because, on the contrary, it brings them closer to us and in a sense places them below us. Their sanctity is given them in order that they may help us and serve us—for the saints are like doctors and nurses who are better than the sick in the sense that they are healthy and possess arts of healing them, and yet they make themselves the servants of the sick and devote their own health and their art to them.

The saints are what they are, not because their sanctity makes them admirable to others, but *because the gift of sainthood makes it possible for them to admire everybody else*. It gives them a clarity of compassion that can find good in the most terrible criminals. It delivers them from the burden of judging others, condemning other men. It teaches them to bring the good out of others by compassion, mercy and pardon. A man becomes a saint not by conviction that he is better than sinners but by the realization that he is one of them, and that all together need the mercy of God!

In humility is the greatest freedom. As long as you have to defend the imaginary self that you think is important, you lose your peace of heart. As soon as you compare that shadow with the shadows of other people, you lose all joy, because you have begun to trade in unrealities, and there is no joy in things that do not exist.

As soon as you begin to take yourself seriously and imagine that your virtues are important because they are yours, you become the prisoner of your own vanity and even your best works will blind and deceive you. Then, in order to defend yourself, you will begin to see sins and faults everywhere in the actions of other men. And the more unreasonable importance you attach to yourself and to your own works, the more you will tend to build up your own idea of yourself by condemning other people. Sometimes virtuous men are also bitter and unhappy, because they have unconsciously come to believe that all their happiness depends on their being more virtuous than others.

When humility delivers a man from attachment to his own works and his own reputation, he discovers that perfect joy is possible only when we have completely forgotten ourselves. And it is only when we pay no more attention to our own deeds and our own reputation and our own excellence that we are at last completely free to serve God in perfection for His own sake alone.

A MAN who is not stripped and poor and naked within his own soul will unconsciously tend to do the works he has to do for his own sake rather than for the glory of God. He will be virtuous not because he loves God's will but because he wants to admire his own virtues. But every moment of the day will bring him some frustration that will make him bitter and impatient and in his impatience he will be discovered.

He has planned to do spectacular things. He cannot conceive himself without a halo. And when the events of his daily life keep reminding him of his own insignificance and mediocrity, he is ashamed, and his pride refuses to swallow a truth at which no sane man should be surprised.

Even the professionally pious, and sometimes the pious most of all, can waste their time in competition with one another, in which nothing is found but misery.

More than once Jesus had to rebuke His Apostles, who were wrangling among themselves and fighting for the first places in His Kingdom. Two of them, James and John, intrigued for the seats on His right and left hand in the Kingdom. It is not unusual, in the lives of saints, to find that saints did not always agree with saints. Peter did not always agree with Paul, or Philip Neri with Charles Borromeo. And sometimes very holy men have been very exasperating people and tiresome to live with. If you do not believe me, perhaps it is because you think that the saints were always perfect, and never had any faults to fight against. But God sometimes permits men to retain certain defects and imperfections, blind-spots and eccentricities, even after they have reached a high degree of sanctity, and because of these things their sanctity remains hidden from them and from other men. If the holiness of all the saints had always been plainly evident to everybody, they would never have been polished and perfected by trial, criticism, humiliation and opposition from the people they lived with.

Be content that you are not yet a saint, even though you realize that the only thing worth living for is sanctity. Then you will be satisfied to let God lead you to sanctity by paths that you cannot understand. You will travel in darkness in which you will no longer be concerned with yourself and no longer compare yourself with other men. Those who have gone by that way have finally found out that sanctity is in everything and that God is all around them. Having given up all desire to compete with other men, they suddenly wake up and find that the joy of God is everywhere, and they are able to exult in the virtues and goodness of others more than ever they could have done in their own. They are so dazzled by the reflection of God in the souls of the men they live with that they no longer have any power to condemn anything they see in another. Even in the greatest sinners they can see virtues and goodness that no one else can find. As for themselves, if they still consider themselves, they no longer dare to compare themselves with others. The idea has now become unthinkable. But it is no longer a source of suffering and lamentation: they have finally reached the point where they take their own insignificance for granted. They are no longer interested in their external selves.

To say that I am made in the image of God is to say that love is the reason for my existence, for God is love.

Love is my true identity. Selflessness is my true self. Love is my true character. Love is my name.

If, therefore, I do anything or think anything or say anything or know anything that is not purely for the love of God, it cannot give me peace, or rest, or fulfilment, or joy.

To find love I must enter into the sanctuary where it is hidden, which is the mystery of God. And to enter into His sanctity I must become holy as He is holy, perfect as He is perfect.

How can I even dare to entertain such a thought? Is it not madness? It is certainly madness if I think I know what the holiness and perfection of God really are in themselves and if I think that there is some way in which I can apply myself to imitating them. I must begin, then, by realizing that the holiness of God is something that is to me, and to all men, utterly mysterious, inscrutable, beyond the highest notion of any kind of perfection, beyond any relevant human statement whatever.

If I am to be "holy" I must therefore be something that I do not understand, something mysterious and hidden, something apparently self-contradictory; for God, in Christ, "emptied Himself." He became a man, and dwelt among sinners. He was considered a sinner. He was put to death as a blasphemer, as one who at least implicitly denied God, as one who revolted against the holiness of God. Indeed, the great question in the trial and condemnation of Christ was precisely the denial of God and the denial of His holiness. So God Himself was put to death on the Cross because He did not measure up to man's conception of His holiness. . . . He was not holy enough, He was not holy in the right way, He was not holy in the way they had been led to expect. Therefore he was not God at all. And, indeed, He was abandoned and forsaken even by Himself. It was as if the Father had denied the Son, as if the Divine Power and mercy had utterly failed.

In dying on the Cross, Christ manifested the holiness of God in apparent contradiction with itself. But in reality this manifestation was the complete denial and rejection of all human ideas of holiness and perfection. The wisdom of God became folly to men, His power manifested itself as weakness, and His holiness was, in their eyes, unholy. But Scripture says that "what is great in the eyes of men is an abomination in the sight of God," and again, "my thoughts are not your thoughts," says God to men.

If, then, we want to seek some way of being holy, we must first of all renounce our own way and our own wisdom. We must "empty ourselves" as He did. We must "deny ourselves" and in some sense make ourselves "nothing" in order that we may live not so much in ourselves as in Him. We must live by a power and a light that seem not to be there. We must live by the strength of an apparent emptiness that is always truly empty and yet never fails to support us at every moment.

This is holiness.

None of this can be achieved by any effort of my own, by any striving of my own, by any competition with other men. It means leaving all the ways that men can follow or understand.

I who am without love cannot become love unless Love identifies me with Himself. But if He sends His own Love, Himself, to act and love in me and in all that I do, then I shall be transformed, I shall discover who I am and shall possess my true identity by losing myself in Him.

And that is what is called sanctity.

9

We are One Man

ONE of the paradoxes of the mystical life is this: that *a man cannot enter into the deepest centre of himself and pass through that centre into God, unless he is able to pass entirely out of himself and empty himself and give himself to other people in the purity of a selfless love.*

And so one of the worst illusions in the life of contemplation would be to try to find God by barricading yourself inside your own soul, shutting out all external reality by sheer concentration and will-power, cutting yourself off from the world and other men by stuffing yourself inside your own mind and closing the door like a turtle.

Fortunately most of the men who try this sort of thing never succeed. For self-hypnotism is the exact opposite of contemplation. We enter into possession of God when He invades all our faculties with His light and His infinite fire. We do not "possess" Him until He takes full possession of us. But this business of doping your mind and isolating yourself from everything that lives merely deadens you. How can fire take possession of what is frozen?

THE more I become identified with God, the more will I be identified with all the others who are identified with Him. His Love will live in all of us. His Spirit will be our One Life, the Life of all of us and Life of God. And we shall love one another and God with the same Love with which He loves us and Himself. This love is God Himself.

Christ prayed that all men might become One as He was One with His Father, in the Unity of the Holy Spirit. Therefore when you and I become what we are really meant to be, we will discover not only that we love one another perfectly but that we are both living in Christ and Christ in us, and we are all One Christ. We will see that it is He who loves in us.

The ultimate perfection of the contemplative life is not a heaven of separate individuals, each one viewing his own private intuition of God; it is a sea of Love which flows through the One Body of all the elect, all the angels and saints, and their contemplation would be incomplete if it were not shared, or if it were shared with fewer souls, or with spirits capable of less vision and less joy.

I will have more joy in heaven and in the contemplation of God, if you are also there to share it with me; and the more of us there will be to share it the greater will be the joy of all. For contemplation is not ultimately perfect unless it is shared. We do not finally taste the full exultation of God's glory until we share His infinite gift of it by overflowing and transmitting glory all over heaven, and seeing God in all the others who are there, and knowing that He is the Life of all of us and that we are all One in Him.

Even on earth it is the same, but in obscurity. This unity is something we cannot yet realize and enjoy except in the darkness of faith. But even here the more we are one with God the more we are united with one another; and the silence of contemplation is deep, rich and endless society, not only with God but with men. The contemplative is not isolated in himself, but liberated from his external and egotistic self by humility and purity of heart—therefore there is no longer any serious obstacle to simple and humble love of other men.

The more we are alone with God the more we are with one another, in darkness, yet a multitude. And the more we go out to one another in work and activity and communication, according to the will and charity of God, the more we are multiplied in Him and yet we are in solitude.

The more we are alone, the more we are together; and the more we are in society, the true society of charity, not of cities and crowds, the more we are alone with Him. For in my soul and in your soul I find the same Christ who is our Life, and He finds Himself in our love, and together we all find Paradise, which is the sharing of His Love for His Father in the Person of Their Spirit.

My true personality will be fulfilled in the Mystical Christ in this one way above all, that through me Christ and His Spirit will be able to love you and all men and God the Father in a way that would be possible in no one else.

Love comes out of God and gathers us to God in order to pour itself back into God through all of us and bring us all back to Him on the tide of His own infinite mercy.

So we all become doors and windows through which God shines back into His own house.

When the Love of God is in me, God is able to love you through me and you are able to love God through me. If my soul were closed to that love, God's love for you and your love for God and God's love for Himself in you and in me would be denied the particular expression which it finds through me and through no other.

Because God's love is in me, it can come to you from a different and special direction that would be closed if He did not live in me, and because His love is in you, it can come to me from a quarter from which it would not otherwise come. And because it is in both of us, God has greater glory. His love is expressed in two more ways in which it would not otherwise be expressed; that is, in two more joys that could not exist without Him.

LET us live in this love and this happiness, you and I and all of us, in the love of Christ and in contemplation, for this is where we find ourselves and one another as we truly are. It is only in this love that we at last become real. For it is here that we most truly share the life of One God in Three Persons.

God in His Trinity of subsistent relations infinitely transcends every shadow of selfishness. For the One God does not subsist apart and alone in His Nature; He subsists as Father and as Son and as Holy Ghost. These Three Persons are one, but apart from them God does not subsist also as One. He is not Three Persons *plus* one nature, therefore four! He is Three Persons, but One God. He is at once infinite solitude (one nature) and perfect society (Three Persons). One Infinite Love in three subsistent relations.

The One God who exists only in Three Persons is a circle of relations in which His infinite reality, Love, is ever identical and ever renewed, always perfect and always total, always beginning and never ending, absolute, everlasting and full.

In the Father the infinite Love of God is always beginning and in the Son it is always full and in the Holy Spirit it is perfect and it is renewed and never ceases to rest in its everlasting source. But if you follow Love forward and backward from Person to Person, you can never track it to a stop, you can never corner it and hold it down and fix it to one of the Persons as if He could appropriate to Himself the fruit of the love of the others. For the One Love of the Three Persons is an infinitely rich giving of Itself which never ends and is never taken, but is always perfectly given, only received in order to be perfectly shared.

It is because the Love of God does not terminate in one self-sufficient *self* that is capable of halting and absorbing it, that the Life and Happiness of God are absolutely infinite and perfect and inexhaustible. Therefore in God there can be no selfishness, because the Three Selves of God are Three subsistent relations of selflessness, overflowing and superabounding in joy in the Gift of their One Life.

The interior life of God is perfect contemplation. Our joy and our life are destined to be nothing but a participation in the Life that is Theirs. In Them we will one day live entirely in God and in one another as the Persons of God live in one another.

10

A Body of Broken Bones

YOU and I and all men were made to find our identity in the One Mystical Christ, in whom we all complete one another "unto a perfect man, unto the measure of the age of the fulness of Christ."

When we all reach that perfection of love which is the contemplation of God in His glory, our inalienable personalities, while remaining eternally distinct, will nevertheless combine into One so that each one of us will find himself in all the others, and God will be the life and reality of all. *Omnia in omnibus Deus.*

God is a consuming Fire. He alone can refine us like gold, and separate us from the slag and dross of our selfish individualities to fuse us into this wholeness of perfect unity that will reflect His own Triune Life forever.

As long as we do not permit His love to consume us entirely and to unite us in Himself, the gold that is in us will be hidden by the rock and dirt which keep us separate from one another.

As long as we are not purified by the love of God and transformed into Him in the union of pure sanctity, we will remain apart from one another, opposed to one another, and union among us will be a precarious and painful thing, full of labour and sorrow and without lasting cohesion.

IN the whole world, throughout the whole of history, even among religious men and among saints, Christ suffers dismemberment.

His physical Body was crucified by Pilate and the Pharisees; His mystical Body is drawn and quartered from age to age by the devils in the agony of that disunion which is bred and vegetates in our souls, prone to selfishness and to sin.

All over the face of the earth the avarice and lust of men breed unceasing divisions among them, and the wounds that tear men from union with one another widen and open out into huge wars. Murder, massacres, revolution, hatred, the slaughter and torture of the bodies and souls of men, the destruction of cities by fire, the starvation of millions, the annihilation of populations and finally the cosmic inhumanity of atomic war: Christ is massacred in His members, torn limb from limb; God is murdered in men.

The history of the world, with the material destruction of cities and nations and people, expresses the interior division that tyrannizes the souls of all men, and even of the saints.

Even the innocent, even those in whom Christ lives by charity, even those who want with their whole heart to love one another, remain divided and separate. Although they are already one in Him, their union is hidden from them, because it still only possesses the secret substance of their souls.

But their minds and their judgments and their desires, their human characters and faculties, their appetites and their ideals are all imprisoned in the slag of an inescapable egotism which pure love has not yet been able to refine.

As long as we are on earth, the love that unites us will bring us suffering by our very contact with one another, because this love is the resetting of a Body of broken bones. Even saints cannot live with saints on this earth without some anguish, without some pain at the differences that come between them.

There are two things which men can do about the pain of disunion with other men. They can love or they can hate.

Hatred recoils from the sacrifice and the sorrow that are the price of this resetting of bones. It refuses the pain of reunion.

There is in every weak, lost and isolated member of the human race an agony of hatred born of his own helplessness, his own isolation. Hatred is the sign and the expression of loneliness, of unworthiness, of insufficiency. And in so far as each one of us is lonely, is unworthy, each one hates himself. Some of us are aware of this self-hatred, and because of it we reproach ourselves and punish ourselves needlessly. Punishment cannot cure the feeling that we are unworthy. There is nothing we can do about it as long as we feel that we are isolated, insufficient, helpless, alone. Others, who are less conscious of their own self-hatred, realize it in a different form by projecting it on to others. There is a proud and self-confident hate, strong and cruel, which enjoys the pleasure of hating, for it is directed outward to the unworthiness of another. But this strong and happy hate does not realize that, like all hate, it destroys and consumes the self that hates, and not the object that is hated. Hate in any form is self-destructive, and even when it triumphs physically it triumphs in its own spiritual ruin.

Strong hate, the hate that takes joy in hating, is strong because it does not believe itself to be unworthy and alone. It feels the support of a justifying God, of an idol of war, an avenging and destroying spirit. From such blood-drinking gods the human race was once liberated, with great toil and terrible sorrow, by the death of a God who delivered Himself to the Cross and suffered the pathological cruelty of His own creatures out of pity for them. In conquering death He opened their eyes to the reality of a love which asks no questions about worthiness, a love which overcomes hatred and destroys death. But men have now come to reject this divine revelation of pardon, and they are consequently returning to the old war gods, the gods that insatiably drink blood and eat the flesh of men. It is easier to serve the hate-gods because they thrive on the worship of collective fanaticism. To serve the hate-gods, one has only to be blinded by collective passion. To serve the God of Love one must be free, one must face the terrible responsibility of the decision to love *in spite of all unworthiness* whether in oneself or in one's neighbour.

It is the rankling, tormenting sense of unworthiness that lies at the root of all hate. The man who is able to hate strongly and with a quiet conscience is one who is complacently blind to all unworthiness in himself and serenely capable of seeing all his own wrongs in someone else. But the man who is aware of his own unworthiness and the unworthiness of his brother is tempted with a subtler and more tormenting kind of hate: the general, searing, nauseating hate of everything and everyone, because everything is tainted with unworthiness, everything is unclean, everything is foul with sin. What this weak hate really is, is weak love. He who cannot love feels unworthy, and at the same time feels that somehow *no one* is worthy. Perhaps he cannot feel love because he thinks he is unworthy of love, and because of that he also thinks no one else is worthy.

The beginning of the fight against hatred, the basic Christian answer to hatred, is not the commandment to love, but what must necessarily come before in order to make the commandment bearable and comprehensible. It is a prior commandment *to believe*. The root of Christian love is not the will to love, but *the faith that one is loved*. The faith that one is loved *by God*. That faith that one is loved by God although unworthy—or, rather, irrespective of one's worth!

In the true Christian vision of God's love, the idea of worthiness loses its significance. Revelation of the mercy of God makes the whole problem of worthiness something almost laughable: the discovery that worthiness is of no special consequence (since no one could ever, by himself, be strictly worthy to be loved with such a love) is a true liberation of the spirit. And until this discovery is made, until this liberation has been brought about by the divine mercy, man is imprisoned in hate.

Humanistic love will not serve. As long as we believe that we hate no one, that we are merciful, that we are kind by our very nature, we deceive ourselves; our hatred is merely smouldering under the grey ashes of complacent optimism. We are apparently at peace with everyone because we think we are worthy. That is to say we have lost the capacity to face the question of unworthiness at all. But when we are delivered by the mercy of God the question no longer has a meaning.

Hatred tries to cure disunion by annihilating those who are not united with us. It seeks peace by the elimination of everybody else but ourselves.

But love, by its acceptance of the pain of reunion, begins to heal all wounds.

If you want to know what is meant by "God's will" in man's life, this is one way to get a good idea of it. "God's will" is certainly found in anything that is required of us in order that we may be united with one another in love. You can call this, if you like, the basic tenet of the Natural Law, which is that we should treat others as we would like them to treat us, that we should not do to another what we would not want another to do to us. In other words, the natural law is simply that we should recognize in every other human being the same nature, the same needs, the same rights, the same destiny as in ourselves. The plainest summary of all the natural law is: to treat other men as if they were men. Not to act as if I alone were a man, and every other human were an animal or a piece of furniture.

Everything that is demanded of me, in order that I may treat every other man effectively as a human being, "is willed for me by God under the natural law." Whether or not I find the formula satisfactory, it is obvious that I cannot live a truly human life if I consistently disobey this fundamental principle.

But I cannot treat other men as men unless I have compassion for them. I must have at least enough compassion to realize that when they suffer they feel somewhat as I do when I suffer. And if for some reason I do not spontaneously feel this kind of sympathy for others, then it is God's will that I do what I can to learn how. I must learn to share with others their joys, their sufferings, their ideas, their needs, their desires. I must learn to do this not only in the cases of those who are of the same class, the same profession, the same race, the same nation as myself, but when men who suffer belong to other groups, even to groups that are regarded as hostile. If I do this, I obey God. If I refuse to do it, I disobey Him. It is not therefore a matter left open to subjective caprice.

Since this is God's will for every man, and since contemplation is a gift not granted to anyone who does not consent to God's will, contemplation is out of the question for anyone who does not try to cultivate compassion for other men.

For Christianity is not merely a doctrine or a system of beliefs, it is Christ living in us and uniting men to one another in His own Life and unity. "I in them, and Thou, Father, in Me, that they may be made perfect in One. . . . And the glory which Thou hast given me I have given them, that they may be One as We also are One." *In hoc cognoscent omnes quia mei estis discipuli, si dilectionem habueritis ad invicem.* "In this shall all men know that you are My disciples—if you have love one for another."

"He that loveth not abideth in death."

IF you regard contemplation principally as a means to escape from the miseries of human life, as a withdrawal from the anguish and the suffering of this struggle for reunion with other men in the charity of Christ, you do not know what contemplation is and you will never find God in your contemplation. For it is precisely in the recovery of our union with our brothers in Christ that we discover God and know Him, for then His life begins to penetrate our souls and His love possesses our faculties and we are able to find out who He is from the experience of His mercy, liberating us from the prison of self-concern.

THERE is only one true flight from the world; it is not an escape from conflict, anguish and suffering, but the flight from disunity and separation, to unity and peace in the love of other men.

What is the "world" that Christ would not pray for, and of which He said that His disciples were in it but not of it? The world is the unquiet city of those who live for themselves and are therefore divided against one another in a struggle that cannot end, for it will go on eternally in hell. It is the city of those who are fighting for possession of limited things and for the monopoly of goods and pleasures that cannot be shared by all.

But if you try to escape from this world merely by leaving the city and hiding yourself in solitude, you will only take the city with you into solitude; and yet you can be entirely out of the world while remaining in the midst of it, if you let God set you free from your own selfishness and if you live for love alone.

For the flight from the world is nothing else but the flight from self-concern. And the man who locks himself up in private with his own selfishness has put himself into a position where the evil within him will either possess him like a devil or drive him out of his head.

That is why it is dangerous to go into solitude merely because you like to be alone.

11

Learn to be Alone

PHYSICAL solitude, exterior silence and real recollection are all morally necessary for anyone who wants to lead a contemplative life, but like everything else in creation they are nothing more than means to an end, and if we do not understand the end we will make a wrong use of the means.

We do not go into the desert to escape people but to learn how to find them; we do not leave them in order to have nothing more to do with them, but to find out the way to do them the most good. But this is only a secondary end.

The one end that includes all others is the love of God.

How can people act and speak as if solitude were a matter of no importance in the interior life? Only those who have never experienced real solitude can glibly declare that it "makes no difference" and that only solitude of the heart really matters! One solitude must lead to the other!

However, the truest solitude is not something outside you, not an absence of men or of sound around you; it is an abyss opening up in the centre of your own soul.

And this abyss of interior solitude is a hunger that will never be satisfied with any created thing.

The only way to find solitude is by hunger and thirst and sorrow and poverty and desire, and the man who has found solitude is empty, as if he had been emptied by death.

He has advanced beyond all horizons. There are no directions left in which he can travel. This is a country whose centre is everywhere and whose circumference is nowhere. You do not find it by travelling but by standing still.

Yet it is in this loneliness that the deepest activities begin. It is here that you discover act without motion, labour that is profound repose, vision in obscurity, and, beyond all desire, a fulfilment whose limits extend to infinity.

Although it is true that this solitude is everywhere, there is a mechanism for finding it that has some reference to actual space, to geography, to physical isolation from the towns and the cities of men.

There should be at least a room, or some corner where no one will find you and disturb you or notice you. You should be able to untether yourself from the world and set yourself free, loosing all the fine strings and strands of tension that bind you, by sight, by sound, by thought, to the presence of other men.

"But thou, when thou shalt pray, enter into thy chamber, and having shut the door, pray to thy Father in secret. . . ."

Once you have found such a place, be content with it, and do not be disturbed if a good reason takes you out of it. Love it, and return to it as soon as you can, and do not be too quick to change it for another.

City churches are sometimes quiet and peaceful solitudes, caves of silence where a man can seek refuge from the intolerable arrogance of the business world. One can be more alone, sometimes, in church than in a room in one's own house. At home, one can always be routed out and disturbed (and one should not resent this, for love sometimes demands it). But in these quiet churches one remains nameless, undisturbed in the shadows, where there are only a few chance, anonymous strangers among the vigil lights, and the curious impersonal postures of the bad statues. The very tastelessness and shabbiness of some churches make them greater solitudes, though churches should not be vulgar. Even if they are, as long as they are dark it makes little difference.

Let there always be quiet, dark churches in which men can take refuge. Places where they can kneel in silence. Houses of God, filled with His silent presence. There, even when they do not know how to pray, at least they can be still and breathe easily. Let there be a place somewhere in which you can breathe naturally, quietly, and not have to take your breath in continuous short gasps. A place where your mind can be idle, and forget its concerns, descend into silence, and worship the Father in secret.

There can be no contemplation where there is no secret.

We have said that the solitude that is important to a contemplative is, above all, an interior and spiritual thing. We have admitted that it is possible to live in deep and peaceful interior solitude even in the midst of the world and its confusion. But this truth is sometimes abused in religion. There are men dedicated to God whose lives are full of restlessness and who have no real desire to be alone. They admit that exterior solitude is good, in theory, but they insist that it is far better to preserve interior solitude while living in the midst of others. In practice, their lives are devoured by activities and strangled with attachments. Interior solitude is impossible for them. They fear it. They do everything they can to escape it. What is worse, they try to draw everyone else into activities as senseless and as devouring as their own. They are great promoters of useless work. They love to organize meetings and banquets and conferences and lectures. They print circulars, write letters, talk for hours on the telephone in order that they may gather a hundred people together in a large room where they will all fill the air with smoke and make a great deal of noise and roar at one another and clap their hands and stagger home at last patting one another on the back with the assurance that they have all done great things to spread the Kingdom of God.

12

The Pure Heart

You will never find interior solitude unless you make some conscious effort to deliver yourself from the desires and the cares and the attachments of an existence in time and in the world.

Do everything you can to avoid the noise and the business of men. Keep as far away as you can from the places where they gather to cheat and insult one another, to exploit one another, to laugh at one another, or to mock one another with their false gestures of friendship. Be glad if you can keep beyond the reach of their radios. Do not bother with their unearthly songs. Do not read their advertisements.

The contemplative life certainly does not demand a self-righteous contempt for the habits and diversions of ordinary people. But nevertheless, no man who seeks liberation and light in solitude, no man who seeks spiritual freedom, can afford to yield passively to all the appeals of a society of salesmen, advertisers and consumers. There is no doubt that life cannot be lived on a human level without certain legitimate pleasures. But to say that all the pleasures which offer themselves to us as necessities are now "legitimate" is quite another story. A natural pleasure is one thing; an unnatural pleasure, forced upon the satiated mind by the importunity of a salesman, is quite another.

It should be accepted as a most elementary human and moral truth that no man can live a fully sane and decent life unless he is able to say "no" on occasion to his natural bodily appetites.

No man who simply eats and drinks whenever he feels like eating and drinking, who smokes whenever he feels the urge to light a cigarette, who gratifies his curiosity and sensuality whenever they are stimulated, can consider himself a free person. He has renounced his spiritual freedom and become the servant of bodily impulse. Therefore his mind and his will are not fully his own. They are under the power of his appetites. And through the medium of his appetites, they are under the control of those who gratify his appetites. Just because he can buy one brand of whisky rather than another, this man deludes himself that he is making a choice; but the fact is that he is a devout servant of a tyrannical ritual. He must reverently buy the bottle, take it home, unwrap it, pour it out for his friends, watch TV, "feel good," talk his silly uninhibited head off, get angry, shout, fight and go to bed in disgust with himself and the world. This becomes a kind of religious compulsion without which he cannot convince himself that he is really alive, really "fulfilling his personality." He is not "sinning" but simply makes an ass of himself, deluding himself that he is real when his compulsions have reduced him to a shadow of a genuine person.

In general, it can be said that no contemplative life is possible without ascetic self-discipline. One must learn to survive without the habit-forming luxuries which get such a hold of men today. I do not say that to be a contemplative one absolutely has to go without smoking or without alcohol, but certainly one must be able to use these things without being dominated by an uncontrolled need for them. There can be no doubt that smoking and drinking are obvious areas for the elementary self-denial without which a life of prayer would be a pure illusion.

I am certainly no judge of television, since I have never watched it. All I know is that there is a sufficiently general agreement, among men whose judgment I respect, that commercial television is degraded, meretricious and absurd. Certainly it would seem that TV could become a kind of unnatural surrogate for contemplation: a completely inert subjection to vulgar images, a descent to a sub-natural passivity rather than an ascent to a supremely active passivity in understanding and love. It would seem that television should be used with extreme care and discrimination by anyone who might hope to take interior life seriously.

Keep your eyes clean and your ears quiet and your mind serene. Breathe God's air. Work, if you can, under His sky.

But if you have to live in a city and work among machines and ride in the subways and eat in a place where the radio makes you deaf with spurious news and where the food destroys your life and the sentiments of those around you poison your heart with boredom, do not be impatient, but accept it as the love of God and as a seed of solitude planted in your soul. If you are appalled by those things, you will keep your appetite for the healing silence of recollection. But meanwhile—keep your sense of compassion for the men who have forgotten the very concept of solitude. You, at least, know that it exists, and that it is the source of peace and joy. You can still hope for such joy. They do not even hope for it any more.

IF you seek escape for its own sake and run away from the world only because it is (as it must be) intensely unpleasant, you will not find peace and you will not find solitude. If you seek solitude merely because it is what you prefer, you will never escape from the world and its selfishness; you will never have the interior freedom that will keep you really alone.

ONE vitally important aspect of solitude is its intimate dependence on chastity. The virtue of chastity is not the complete renunciation of all sex, but simply the right use of sex. This means, according to most of the great religious traditions of the world, the restriction of all sex to married life, and, within the married state, to certain ordinate norms.

Nowhere is self-denial more important than in the area of sex, because this is the most difficult of all natural appetites to control and one whose undisciplined gratification completely blinds the human spirit to all interior light.

Sex is by no means to be regarded as an evil. It is a natural good, willed by God, and entering into the mystery of God's love and God's mercy towards men. But though sex may not be evil in itself, inordinate attachment to sexual pleasure, especially outside of marriage, is one of man's most frequent and pitiable weaknesses. Indeed, it is so common that most people today simply believe that sex cannot be fully controlled—that it is not really possible for a normal human being to abstain from it completely. Hence they assume that one should simply resign himself to the inevitable and cease worrying about it.

One must certainly agree that pathological guilt about sex is no help at all in helping men to get control of passion. However, self-control is not only desirable but altogether possible and it is essential for the contemplative life. It demands considerable effort, watchfulness, patience, humility and trust in divine grace. But the very struggle for chastity teaches us to rely on a spiritual power higher than our own nature, and this is an indispensable preparation for interior prayer. Furthermore, chastity is not possible without ascetic self-sacrifice in many other areas. It demands a certain amount of fasting, it requires a very temperate and well-ordered life, modesty, restraint of curiosity, moderation of one's aggressivity, and many other virtues.

Perfect chastity establishes one in a state of spiritual solitude, peace, tranquillity, clarity, gentleness and joy in which one is fully disposed for meditation and contemplative prayer.

13

The Moral Theology of
the Devil

THE devil has a whole system of theology and philosophy,
which will explain, to anyone who will listen, that
created things are evil, that men are evil, that God created evil
and that He directly wills that men should suffer evil. According to the devil, God rejoices in the suffering of men and, in
fact, the whole universe is full of misery because God has willed
and planned it that way.

Indeed, says this system of theology, God the Father took
real pleasure in delivering His Son to His murderers, and God
the Son came to earth because He wanted to be punished by the
Father. Both of them together seek nothing more than to
punish and persecute their faithful ones. As a matter of fact, in
creating the world God had clearly in mind that man would
inevitably sin and it was almost as if the world were created in
order that man might sin, so that God would have an opportunity to manifest His justice.

So, according to the devil, the first thing created was really
hell—as if everything else were, in some sense, for the sake of
hell. Therefore the devotional life of those who are "faithful"
to this kind of theology consists above all in an obsession with
evil. As if there were not already enough evils in the world,
they multiply prohibitions and make new rules, binding
everything with thorns, so that man may not escape evil and
punishment. For they would have him bleed from morning to

night, though even with so much blood there is no remission of sin! The Cross, then, is no longer a sign of mercy (for mercy has no place in such a theology), it is the sign that Law and Justice have utterly triumphed, as if Christ had said: "I came not to destroy the Law but to be destroyed by it." For this, according to the devil, is the only way in which the Law could really and truly be "fulfilled." Not love but punishment is the fulfilment of the Law. The Law must devour everything, even God. Such is this theology of punishment, hatred and revenge. He who would live by such a dogma must rejoice in punishment. He may, indeed, successfully evade punishment himself by "playing ball" with the Law and the Lawgiver. But he must take good care that others do not avoid suffering. He must occupy his mind with their present and future punishment. The Law must triumph. There must be no mercy.

This is the chief mark of the theology of hell, for in hell there is everything but mercy. That is why God Himself is absent from hell. Mercy is the manifestation of His presence.

THE theology of the devil is for those who, for one reason or another, whether because they are perfect, or because they have come to an agreement with the Law, no longer need any mercy. With them (O grim joy!) God is "satisfied." So too is the devil. It is quite an achievement, to please everybody!

The people who listen to this sort of thing, and absorb it, and enjoy it, develop a notion of the spiritual life which is a kind of hypnosis of evil. The concepts of sin, suffering, damnation, punishment, the justice of God, retribution, the end of the world and so on, are things over which they smack their lips with unspeakable pleasure. Perhaps this is because they derive a deep, subconscious comfort from the thought that many other people will fall into the hell which they themselves are going to escape. And how do they know they are going to escape it?

They cannot give any definite reason except for the fact that they feel a certain sense of relief at the thought that all this punishment is prepared for practically everyone but themselves.

This feeling of complacency is what they refer to as "faith," and it constitutes a kind of conviction that they are "saved."

THE devil makes many disciples by preaching against sin. He convinces them of the great evil of sin, induces a crisis of guilt by which "God is satisfied," and after that he lets them spend the rest of their lives meditating on the intense sinfulness and evident reprobation of other men.

THE moral theology of the devil starts out with the principle: "Pleasure is sin." Then he goes on to work it the other way: "All sin is pleasure."

After that he points out that pleasure is practically unavoidable and that we have a natural tendency to do things that please us, from which he reasons that all our natural tendencies are evil and that our nature is evil in itself. And he leads us to the conclusion that no one can possibly avoid sin, since pleasure is inescapable.

After that, to make sure that no one will try to escape or avoid sin, he adds that what is unavoidable cannot be a sin. Then the whole concept of sin is thrown out the window as irrelevant, and people decide that there is nothing left except to live for pleasure, and in that way pleasures that are naturally good become evil by de-ordination and lives are thrown away in unhappiness and sin.

IT sometimes happens that men who preach most vehemently about evil and the punishment of evil, so that they seem to have practically nothing else on their minds except sin, are really unconscious haters of other men. They think the world does not appreciate them, and this is their way of getting even.

THE devil is not afraid to preach the will of God provided he can preach it in his own way.

The argument goes something like this: "God wills you to do what is right. But you have an interior attraction which tells you, by a nice warm glow of satisfaction, what is right. Therefore, if others try to interfere and make you do something that does not produce this comfortable sense of interior satisfaction, quote Scripture, tell them that you ought to obey God rather than men, and then go ahead and do your own will, do the thing that gives you that nice, warm glow."

THE theology of the devil is really not theology but magic. "Faith" in this theology is really not the acceptance of a God who reveals Himself as mercy. It is a psychological, subjective "force" which applies a kind of violence to reality in order to change it according to one's own whims. Faith is a kind of supereffective wishing: a mastery that comes from a special, mysteriously dynamic will power that is generated by "profound convictions." By virtue of this wonderful energy one can exert a persuasive force even on God Himself and bend His will to one's own will. By this astounding new dynamic soul force of faith (which any quack can develop in you for an appropriate remuneration) you can turn God into a means to your own ends. We become civilized medicine men, and God becomes our servant. Though He is terrible in His own right, He respects our sorcery, He allows Himself to be tamed by it. He will appreciate our dynamism, and will reward it with success in everything we attempt. We will become popular because we have "faith." We will be rich because we have "faith." All our national enemies will come and lay down their arms at our feet because we have "faith." Business will boom all over the world, and we will be able to make money out of everything and everyone under the sun because of the charmed life we lead. We have faith.

But there is a subtle dialectic in all this, too.

We hear that faith does everything. So we close our eyes and strain a bit, to generate some "soul force." We believe. We believe.

Nothing happens.

We close our eyes again, and generate some more soul force. The devil likes us to generate soul force. He helps us to generate plenty of it. We are just gushing with soul force.

But nothing happens.

So we go on with this until we become disgusted with the whole business. We get tired of "generating soul force." We get tired of this "faith" that does not do anything to change reality. It does not take away our anxieties, our conflicts, it leaves us a prey to uncertainty. It does not lift all responsibilities off our shoulders. Its magic is not so effective after all. It does not thoroughly convince us that God is satisfied with us, or even that we are satisfied with ourselves (though in this, it is true, some people's faith is often quite effective).

Having become disgusted with faith, and therefore with God, we are now ready for the Totalitarian Mass Movement that will pick us up on the rebound and make us happy with war, with the persecution of "inferior races" or of enemy classes, or generally speaking, with actively punishing someone who is different from ourselves.

ANOTHER characteristic of the devil's moral theology is the exaggeration of all distinctions between this and that, good and evil, right and wrong. These distinctions become irreducible divisions. No longer is there any sense that we might perhaps

all be more or less at fault, and that we might be expected to
take upon our own shoulders the wrongs of others by for-
giveness, acceptance, patient understanding and love, and thus
help one another to find the truth. On the contrary, in the
devil's theology, the important thing is to be absolutely right
and to prove that everybody else is absolutely wrong. This does
not exactly make for peace and unity among men, because it
means that everyone wants to be absolutely right himself or
to attach himself to another who is absolutely right. And in
order to prove their rightness they have to punish and eliminate
those who are wrong. Those who are wrong, in turn, convinced that they are right . . . etc.

Finally, as might be expected, the moral theology of the
devil grants an altogether unusual amount of importance to . . .
the devil. Indeed one soon comes to find out that he is the very
centre of the whole system. That he is behind everything. That
he is moving everybody in the world except ourselves. That
he is out to get even us. And that there is every chance of his
doing so because, it now appears, his power is equal to that of
God, or even perhaps superior to it. . . .

In one word, the theology of the devil is purely and simply
that the devil is god.

14

Integrity

MANY poets are not poets for the same reason that many religious men are not saints: they never succeed in being themselves. They never get around to being the particular poet or the particular monk they are intended to be by God. They never become the man or the artist who is called for by all the circumstances of their individual lives.

They waste their years in vain efforts to be some other poet, some other saint. For many absurd reasons, they are convinced that they are obliged to become somebody else who died two hundred years ago and who lived in circumstances utterly alien to their own.

They wear out their minds and bodies in a hopeless endeavour to have somebody else's experiences or write somebody else's poems or possess somebody else's spirituality.

There can be an intense egoism in following everybody else. People are in a hurry to magnify themselves by imitating what is popular—and too lazy to think of anything better.

Hurry ruins saints as well as artists. They want quick success and they are in such haste to get it that they cannot take time to be true to themselves. And when the madness is upon them they argue that their very haste is a species of integrity.

IN great saints you find that perfect humility and perfect integrity coincide. The two turn out to be practically the same thing. The saint is unlike everybody else precisely because he is humble.

As far as the accidentals of this life are concerned, humility can be quite content with whatever satisfies the general run of men. But that does not mean that the essence of humility consists in being just like everybody else. On the contrary, humility consists in being precisely the person you actually are before God, and since no two people are alike, if you have the humility to be yourself you will not be like anyone else in the whole universe. But this individuality will not necessarily assert itself on the surface of everyday life. It will not be a matter of mere appearances, or opinions, or tastes, or ways of doing things. It is something deep in the soul.

To the truly humble man the ordinary ways and customs and habits of men are not a matter for conflict. The saints do not get excited about the things that people eat and drink, wear on their bodies, or hang on the walls of their houses. To make conformity or non-conformity with others in these accidents a matter of life and death is to fill your interior life with confusion and noise. Ignoring all this as indifferent, the humble man takes whatever there is in the world that helps him to find God and leaves the rest aside.

He is able to see quite clearly that what is useful to him may be useless for somebody else, and what helps others to be saints might ruin him. That is why humility brings with it a deep refinement of spirit, a peacefulness, a tact and a common sense without which there is no sane morality.

It is not humility to insist on being someone that you are not. It is as much as saying that you know better than God who you are and who you ought to be. How do you expect to arrive at the end of your own journey if you take the road to another man's city? How do you expect to reach your own perfection by leading somebody else's life? His sanctity will never be yours; you must have the humility to work out your own salvation in a darkness where you are absolutely alone. . . .

And so it takes heroic humility to be yourself and to be nobody but the man, or the artist, that God intended you to be.

You will be made to feel that your honesty is only pride. This is a serious temptation because you can never be sure whether you are being true to your true self or only building up a defence for the false personality that is the creature of your own appetite for esteem.

But the greatest humility can be learned from the anguish of keeping your balance in such a position: of continuing to be yourself without getting tough about it and without asserting your false self against the false selves of other people.

PERFECTION is not something you can acquire like a hat—by walking into a place and trying on several and walking out again ten minutes later with one on your head that fits. Yet people sometimes enter monasteries with that idea.

They are eager to get the first available system fitted on to them and to spend the rest of their lives walking around with the thing on their heads.

They devour books of piety indiscriminately, not stopping to consider how much of what they read applies, or can be applied, to their own lives. Their chief concern is to acquire as many externals as possible, and to decorate their persons with the features they have so rapidly come to associate with perfection. And they walk around in clothes cut to the measure of other people and other situations.

If they do this job thoroughly, their spiritual disguises are apt to be much admired. Like successful artists, they become commercial. After that there is not much hope for them. They are good people, yes; but they are out of place and much of their well-intentioned energy will only be wasted. They have become satisfied with their own brand of sanctity, and with the perfection they have woven for themselves out of their own imaginations.

Such "sanctity" may perhaps be only the fruit of mutual flattery. The "perfection" of the holy one is something that reassures his neighbours by confirming them in their own prejudices, and by enabling them to forget what is lacking in their own communal morality. It makes them all feel that they are "right," that they are on the right way, and that God is "satisfied" with their collective way of life. Therefore nothing needs to be changed. But anyone who opposes this situation is wrong. The sanctity of the "saint" is there to justify the complete elimination of those who are "unholy"—that is, those who do not conform.

So too in art, or literature. The "best" poets are those who happen to succeed in a way that flatters our current prejudice about what constitutes good poetry. We are very exacting about the standards that they have set up, and we cannot even consider a poet who writes in some other slightly different way, whose idiom is not quite the same. We do not read him. We do not dare to, for if we were discovered to have done so, we would fall from grace. We would be excommunicated.

A clever kind of insolent servility, a peculiar combination of ambition, stubbornness and flexibility, a "third ear" keenly attuned to the subtlest modulations of the fashionable cliché— with all this you can pass as a saint or a genius if you conform to the right group. You will be blamed in a way that gives you great pleasure, because the blame will come from an out-group by which to be blamed is praise. You may not be enthusiastically praised, even by your own friends. But they know exactly what you are driving at. They fully accept your standards. They dig you. You are canonized. You are the embodiment of their own complacency.

ONE of the first signs of a saint may well be the fact that other people do not know what to make of him. In fact, they are not sure whether he is crazy or only proud; but it must at least be pride to be haunted by some individual ideal which nobody but God really comprehends. And he has inescapable difficulties in applying all the abstract norms of "perfection" to his own life. He cannot seem to make his life fit in with the books.

Sometimes his case is so bad that no monastery will keep him. He has to be dismissed, sent back to the world like Benedict Joseph Labre, who wanted to be a Trappist and a Carthusian and succeeded in neither. He finally ended up as a tramp. He died in some street in Rome.

And yet the only canonized saint, venerated by the whole Church, who has lived either as a Cistercian or a Carthusian since the Middle Ages is St. Benedict Joseph Labre.

15

Sentences

To hope is to risk frustration. Therefore, make up your mind to risk frustration.

Do not be one of those who, rather than risk failure, never attempt anything.

THE concept of "virtue" does not appeal to men, because they are no longer interested in becoming good. Yet if you tell them that St. Thomas talks about virtues as "habits of the practical intellect," they may, perhaps, pay some attention to your words. They are pleased with the thought of anything that would seem to make them clever. It gets them something.

OUR minds are like crows. They pick up everything that glitters, no matter how uncomfortable our nests get with all that metal in them.

THE devils are very pleased with a soul that comes out of its dry house and shivers in the rain for no other reason than that the house is dry.

I HAVE very little idea of what is going on in the world, but occasionally I happen to see some of the things they are drawing and writing there and it gives me the conviction that they are all living in ash cans. It makes me glad I cannot hear what they are singing.

IF a writer is so cautious that he never writes anything that cannot be criticized, he will never write anything that can be read. If you want to help other people you have got to make up your mind to write things that some men will condemn.

YOU cannot be a man of faith unless you know how to doubt. You cannot believe in God unless you are capable of questioning the authority of prejudice, even though that prejudice may seem to be religious. Faith is not blind conformity to a prejudice —a "pre-judgment." It is a decision, a judgment that is fully and deliberately taken in the light of a truth that cannot be proven. It is not merely the acceptance of a decision that has been made by somebody else.

A "FAITH" that merely confirms us in opinionatedness and self-complacency may well be an expression of theological doubt. True faith is never merely a source of spiritual comfort. It may indeed bring peace, but before it does so it must involve us in struggle. A "faith" that avoids this struggle is really a temptation against true faith.

MEMORY is corrupted and ruined by a crowd of "memories." If I am going to have a true memory, there are a thousand things that must first be forgotten. Memory is not fully itself when it reaches only in the past. A memory that is not alive to the present does not "remember" the here and now, does not "remember" its true identity, is not memory at all. He who remembers nothing but facts and past events, and is never brought back into the present, is a victim of amnesia.

WE are so convinced that past evils must repeat themselves that we make them repeat themselves. We dare not risk a new life in which the evils of the past are totally forgotten; a new life seems to imply new evils, and we would rather face evils that are already familiar. Hence we cling to the evil that has already become ours, and renew it from day to day, until we become identified with it and change is no longer thinkable.

WHAT about the men who run about the countryside painting signs that say "Jesus saves" and "Prepare to meet God!" Have you ever seen one of them? I have not, but I often try to imagine them, and I wonder what goes on in their minds. Strange, their signs do not make me think of Jesus, but of *them*. Or perhaps it is "their Jesus" who gets in the way and makes all thought of Jesus impossible. They wish to force *their* Jesus upon us, and He is perhaps only a projection of themselves. They seem to be at times threatening the world with judgment and at other times promising it mercy. But are they asking simply to be loved and recognized and valued, for themselves? In any case, their Jesus is quite different from mine. But because their concept is different, should I reject it in horror, with distaste? If I do, perhaps I reject something in my own self that I no longer recognize to be there. And in any case, if I can tolerate their Jesus then I can accept and love *them*. Or I can at least conceive of doing so. Let not their Jesus be a barrier between us, or *they* will be a barrier between us and Jesus.

THAT which is oldest is most young and most new. There is nothing so ancient and so dead as human novelty. The "latest" is always stillborn. It never even manages to arrive. What is really *new* is what was there all the time. I say, not what has *repeated itself* all the time; the really "new" is that which, at every moment, springs freshly into new existence. This newness never repeats itself. Yet it is so old it goes back to the earliest beginning. It is the very beginning itself, which speaks to us.

For "primitives," past and future are in the present. For "moderns," the present is either in the future or in the past. They have no present, only a permanently self-repeating state of confusion. But the confusion is punctuated by sharp, practical noises: people announce the date, the hour, the minute of the day. At every instant they exclaim that something important has just taken place, or is just about to take place. Indeed, one is able to "be present" at great events that are taking place. But in the grey, sloppy confusion of jumbled instants there is no longer a present and events are without character or meaning to those who seem to be participating in them. Instead of engaging in meaningful action, we bombard one another with statements and declarations, with interpretations of what has happened, is happening, or is about to happen. We keep telling each other the time, as though time itself would cease to exist if we stopped talking about it. Well, maybe it would! . . .

The most difficult and the most necessary of renunciations: to give up resentment. This is almost impossible, for without resentment modern life would probably cease to be human at all. Resentment enables us to survive the absurdity of existence in a modern city. It is the last-ditch stand of freedom in the midst of confusion. The confusion is inescapable, but at least we can refuse to accept it, we can say "No." We can live in a state of mute protest.

But if resentment is a device which enables man to survive, it does not enable him, necessarily, to survive healthily. It is not a real exercise of freedom. It is not a genuine expression of personal integrity. It is the mute, animal protest of a mistreated psychophysical organism. Driven too far it becomes mental sickness; that, too, is an "adaptation" in its own way. But it is an adaptation by way of escape.

THE problem is to learn how to renounce resentment without selling out to the organization people who want everyone to accept absurdity and moral anarchy in a spirit of uplift and willing complicity. Few men are strong enough to find the solution. A monastery is not necessarily the right answer; there is resentment in monasteries also, and for the same reason that there is resentment anywhere else.

IF you want to renounce resentment you have to renounce the shadow self that feels itself menaced by the confusion without which it cannot subsist. This is the problem: having to live in complete servile dependence upon a system, an organization, a society, or a person that one despises or hates. To live in such dependence and yet to be compelled, by one's own attachment to what appears to be an "identity," to seemingly approve and accept what one hates. To have an "I" that is essentially servile and dependent, and which expresses its servility by constantly lauding and flattering the tyrant to whom it remains unwillingly, yet necessarily, subject.

ULTIMATELY it is a question of servility. And servility may be a purely subjective condition. It may be that we regard ourselves as slaves, even when we are not dominated by anybody. It may be that we are not capable of existing except in a state in which we imagine ourselves to be under domination. In that event, resentment may help to make the situation acceptable, but it can never make us healthy. It is only a justification, a pretence that we would be free if we could. But what if we discovered that we are, in fact, already free?

IT is not that someone else is preventing you from living happily; you yourself do not know what you want. Rather than admit this, you pretend that someone is keeping you from exercising your liberty. Who is this? It is you yourself.

But as long as you pretend to live in pure autonomy, as your own master, without even a god to rule you, you will inevitably live as the servant of another man or as the alienated member of an organization. Paradoxically it is the acceptance of God that makes you free and delivers you from human tyranny, for when you serve Him you are no longer permitted to alienate your spirit in human servitude. God did not *invite* the Children of Israel to leave the slavery of Egypt: He *commanded* them to do so.

The poet enters into himself in order to create. The contemplative enters into God in order to be created.

A Catholic poet should be an apostle by being first of all a poet, not try to be a poet by being first of all an apostle. For if he presents himself to people as a poet, he is going to be judged as a poet and if he is not a good one his apostolate will be ridiculed.

If you write for God you will reach many men and bring them joy.

If you write for men—you may make some money and you may give someone a little joy and you may make a noise in the world, for a little while.

If you write only for yourself you can read what you yourself have written and after ten minutes you will be so disgusted you will wish that you were dead.

16

The Root of War is Fear

A T the root of all war is fear: not so much the fear men have of one another as the fear they have of *everything*. It is not merely that they do not trust one another; they do not even trust themselves. If they are not sure when someone else may turn around and kill them, they are still less sure when they may turn around and kill themselves. They cannot trust anything, because they have ceased to believe in God.

IT is not only our hatred of others that is dangerous but also and above all our hatred of ourselves: particularly that hatred of ourselves which is too deep and too powerful to be consciously faced. For it is this which makes us see our own evil in others and unable to see it in ourselves.

When we see crime in others, we try to correct it by destroying them or at least putting them out of sight. It is easy to identify the sin with the sinner when he is someone other than our own self. In ourselves, it is the other way round; we see the sin, but we have great difficulty in shouldering responsibility for it. We find it very hard to identify our sin with our own will and our own malice. On the contrary, we naturally tend to interpret our immoral act as an involuntary mistake, or as the malice of a spirit in us that is other than ourself. Yet at the same time we are fully aware that others do not make this convenient distinction for us. The acts that have been done by us are, in their eyes, "our" acts and they hold us fully responsible.

What is more, we tend unconsciously to ease ourselves still more of the burden of guilt that is in us, by passing it on to somebody else. When I have done wrong, and have excused myself by attributing the wrong to "another" who is unaccountably "in me," my conscience is not yet satisfied. There is still too much left to be explained. The "other in myself" is too close to home. The temptation is, then, to account for my fault by seeing an equivalent amount of evil in someone else. Hence I minimize my own sins and compensate for doing so by exaggerating the faults of others.

As if this were not enough, we make the situation much worse by artificially intensifying our sense of evil, and by increasing our propensity to feel guilt even for things which are not in themselves wrong. In all these ways we build up such an obsession with evil[1], both in ourselves and in others, that we waste all our mental energy trying to account for this evil, to punish it, to exorcize it, or to get rid of it in any way we can. We drive ourselves mad with our preoccupation and in the end there is no outlet left but violence. We have to destroy something or someone. By that time we have created for ourselves a suitable enemy, a scapegoat in whom we have invested all the evil in the world. He is the cause of every wrong. He is the fomenter of all conflict. If he can only be destroyed, conflict will cease, evil will be done with, there will be no more war.

This kind of fictional thinking is especially dangerous when it is supported by a whole elaborate pseudo-scientific structure of myths, like those which Marxists have adopted as their ersatz for religion. But it is certainly no less dangerous when it operates in the vague, fluid, confused and unprincipled opportunism which substitutes in the West for religion, for philosophy and even for mature thought.

D

WHEN the whole world is in moral confusion, when no one knows any longer what to think, and when, in fact, everybody is running away from the responsibility of thinking, when man makes rational thought about moral issues absurd by exiling himself entirely from realities into the realm of fictions, and when he expends all his efforts in constructing more fictions with which to account for his ethical failures, then it becomes clear that the world cannot be saved from global war and global destruction by the mere efforts and good intentions of peacemakers. In actual fact, everyone is becoming more and more aware of the widening gulf between good purposes and bad results, between efforts to make peace and the growing likelihood of war. It seems that no matter how elaborate and careful the planning, all attempts at international dialogue end in more and more ludicrous failures. In the end no one has any more faith in those who even attempt the dialogue. On the contrary, the negotiators, with all their pathetic good will, become the objects of contempt and of hatred. It is the "men of good will," the men who have made their poor efforts to do something about peace, who will in the end be the most mercilessly reviled, crushed, and destroyed as victims of the universal self-hate of man which they have unfortunately only increased by the failure of their good intentions.

Perhaps we still have a basically superstitious tendency to associate failure with dishonesty and guilt—failure being interpreted as "punishment." Even if a man starts out with good intentions, if he fails we tend to think he was somehow "at fault." If he was not guilty, he was at least "wrong." And "being wrong" is something we have not yet learned to face with equanimity and understanding. We either condemn it with god-like disdain or forgive it with god-like condescension. We do not manage to accept it with human compassion, humility and identification. Thus we never see the one truth that would help us begin to solve our ethical and political problems: that we are *all* more or less wrong, that we are *all* at fault, *all* limited and obstructed by our mixed motives, our self-deception, our greed, our self-righteousness and our tendency to aggressivity and hypocrisy.

IN our refusal to accept the partially good intentions of others and work with them (of course prudently and with resignation to the inevitable imperfection of the result) we are unconsciously proclaiming our own malice, our own intolerance, our own lack of realism, our own ethical and political quackery.

Perhaps in the end the first real step towards peace would be a realistic acceptance of the fact that our political ideals are perhaps to a great extent illusions and fictions to which we cling out of motives that are not always perfectly honest: that because of this we prevent ourselves from seeing any good or any practicability in the political ideals of our enemies—which may, of course, be in many ways even more illusory and dishonest than our own. We will never get anywhere unless we can accept the fact that politics is an inextricable tangle of good and evil motives in which, perhaps, the evil predominate but where one must continue to hope doggedly in what little good can still be found.

But someone will say: "If we once recognize that we are all equally wrong, all political action will instantly be paralysed. We can only act when we assume that we are in the right." On the contrary, I believe the basis for valid political action can only be the recognition that the true solution to our problems is *not* accessible to any one isolated party or nation but that all must arrive at it by working together.

I DO not mean to encourage the guilt-ridden thinking that is always too glad to be "wrong" in everything. This too is an

evasion of responsibility, because every form of oversimplifica-
tion tends to make decisions ultimately meaningless. We must
try to accept ourselves, whether individually or collectively,
not only as perfectly good or perfectly bad, but in our mysterious, unaccountable mixture of good and evil. We have to
stand by the modicum of good that is in us without exaggerating it. We have to defend our real rights, because unless we
respect our own rights we will certainly not respect the rights
of others. But at the same time we have to recognize that we
have wilfully or otherwise trespassed on the rights of others.
We must be able to admit this not only as the result of self-
examination, but when it is pointed out unexpectedly, and
perhaps not too gently, by somebody else.

These principles which govern personal moral conduct,
which makes harmony possible in small social units like the
family, also apply in the wider area of the state and in the whole
community of nations. It is, however, quite absurd, in our
present situation or in any other, to expect these principles to
be universally accepted as the result of moral exhortations.
There is very little hope that the world will be run according
to them, all of a sudden, as a result of some hypothetical
change of heart on the part of politicians. It is useless and even
laughable to base political thought on the faint hope of a
purely contingent and subjective moral illumination in the
hearts of the world's leaders. But outside of political thought
and action, in the religious sphere, it is not only permissible to
hope for such a mysterious consummation, but it is necessary
to pray for it. We can and must believe not so much that the
mysterious light of God can "convert" the ones who are
mostly responsible for the world's peace, but at least that they
may, in spite of their obstinacy and their prejudices, be
guarded against fatal error.

IT would be sentimental folly to expect men to trust one another when they obviously cannot be trusted. But at least they can learn to trust God. They can bring themselves to see that the mysterious power of God can, quite independently of human malice and error, protect men unaccountably against themselves, and that He can always turn evil into good, though perhaps not always in a sense that would be understood by the preachers of sunshine and uplift. If they can trust and love God, who is infinitely wise and who rules the lives of men, permitting them to use their freedom even to the point of almost incredible abuse, they can love men who are evil. They can learn to love them even in their sin, as God has loved them. If we can love the men we cannot trust (without trusting them foolishly) and if we can to some extent share the burden of their sin by identifying ourselves with them, then perhaps there is some hope of a kind of peace on earth, based not on the wisdom and the manipulations of men but on the inscrutable mercy of God.

FOR only love—which means humility—can exorcize the fear which is at the root of all war.

What is the use of postmarking our mail with exhortations to "pray for peace" and then spending billions of dollars on atomic submarines, thermonuclear weapons, and ballistic missiles? This, I would think, would certainly be what the New Testament calls "mocking God"—and mocking Him far more effectively than the atheists do. The culminating horror of the joke is that we are piling up these weapons to protect ourselves against atheists who, quite frankly, believe there is no God and are convinced that one has to rely on bombs and missiles since nothing else offers any real security. Is it then because we have so much trust in the power of God that we are intent upon utterly destroying these people before

they can destroy us? Even at the risk of destroying ourselves
at the same time?

I DO not mean to imply that prayer excludes the simultaneous
use of ordinary human means to accomplish a naturally good
and justifiable end. One can very well pray for a restoration
of physical health and at the same time take medicine prescribed
by a doctor. In fact, a believer should normally do both.
And there would seem to be a reasonable and right proportion
between the use of these two means to the same end.

But consider the utterly fabulous amount of money,
planning, energy, anxiety and care which go into the produc-
tion of weapons which almost immediately become obsolete
and have to be scrapped. Contrast all this with the pitiful little
gesture "pray for peace" piously cancelling our four-cent
stamps! Think, too, of the disproportion between our piety
and the enormous act of murderous destruction which we at
the same time countenance without compunction and without
shame! It does not even seem to enter our minds that there
might be some incongruity in praying to the God of peace,
the God who told us to love one another as He had loved us,
who warned us that they who took the sword would perish
by it, and at the same time planning to annihilate not thousands
but millions of civilians and soldiers, men, women and children
without discrimination, even with the almost infallible
certainty of inviting the same annihilation for ourselves!

It may make sense for a sick man to pray for health and then
take medicine, but I fail to see any sense at all in his praying
for health and then drinking poison.

WHEN I pray for peace I pray God to pacify not only the
Russians and the Chinese but above all my own nation and
myself. When I pray for peace I pray to be protected not only

from the Reds but also from the folly and blindness of my own country. When I pray for peace, I pray not only that the enemies of my country may cease to want war, but above all that my own country will cease to do the things that make war inevitable. In other words, when I pray for peace I am not just praying that the Russians will give up without a struggle and let us have our own way. I am praying that both we and the Russians may somehow be restored to sanity and learn how to work out our problems, as best we can, together, instead of preparing for global suicide.

I am fully aware that this sounds utterly sentimental, archaic and out of tune with an age of science. But I would like to submit that pseudo-scientific thinking in politics and sociology have so far had much less than this to offer. One thing I would like to add in all fairness is that the atomic scientists themselves are quite often the ones most concerned about the ethics of the situation, and that they are among the few who dare to open their mouths from time to time and say something about it.

But who on earth listens?

IF men really wanted peace they would sincerely ask God for it and He would give it to them. But why should He give the world a peace which it does not really desire? The peace the world pretends to desire is really no peace at all.

To some men peace merely means the liberty to exploit other people without fear of retaliation or interference. To others peace means the freedom to rob others without interruption. To still others it means the leisure to devour the goods of the earth without being compelled to interrupt their pleasures to feed those whom their greed is starving. And to practically everybody peace simply means the absence of any physical violence that might cast a shadow over lives devoted to the satisfaction of their animal appetites for comfort and pleasure.

Many men like these have asked God for what they thought was "peace" and wondered why their prayer was not answered. They could not understand that it actually *was* answered. God left them with what they desired, for their idea of peace was only another form of war. The "cold war" is simply the normal consequence of our corrupt idea of a peace based on a policy of "every man for himself" in ethics, economics and political life. It is absurd to hope for a solid peace based on fictions and illusions!

So instead of loving what you think is peace, love other men and love God above all. And instead of hating the people you think are warmakers, hate the appetites and the disorder in your own soul, which are the causes of war. If you love peace, then hate injustice, hate tyranny, hate greed—but hate these things *in yourself*, not in another.

17

Hell as Hatred

HELL is where no one has anything in common with anybody else except the fact that they all hate one another and cannot get away from one another and from themselves.

They are all thrown together in their fire and each one tries to thrust the others away from him with a huge, impotent hatred. And the reason why they want to be free of one another is not so much that they hate what they see in others, as that they know others hate what they see in them: and all recognize in one another what they detest in themselves, selfishness and impotence, agony, terror and despair.

The tree is known by its fruits. If you want to understand the social and political history of modern man, study hell.

And yet the world, with all its wars, is not yet hell. And history, however terrible, has another and a deeper meaning. For it is not the evil of history that is its significance and it is not by the evil of our time that our time can be understood. In the furnace of war and hatred, the City of those who love one another is drawn and fused together in the heroism of charity under suffering, while the city of those who hate everything is scattered and dispersed and its citizens are cast out in every direction, like sparks, smoke and flame.

OUR God also is a consuming fire. And if we, by love, become transformed into Him and burn as He burns, His fire will be our everlasting joy. But if we refuse His love and remain in the coldness of sin and opposition to Him and to other men then will His fire (by our own choice rather than His) become our everlasting enemy, and Love, instead of being our joy, will become our torment and our destruction.

WHEN we love God's will we find Him and own His joy in all things. But when we are against God, that is, when we love ourselves more than Him, all things become our enemies. They cannot help refusing us the lawless satisfaction our selfishness demands of them because the infinite unselfishness of God is the law of every created essence and is printed in everything that He has made. His creatures can only be friends with His unselfishness. If, in men, they find selfishness, then they hate, fear and resist it—until they are tamed and reduced to passivity by it. But the Desert Fathers believed one of the marks of the saint was that he could live at peace with lions and serpents, with nothing to fear from them.

THERE is nothing interesting about sin, or about evil as evil.

Evil is not a positive entity but the absence of a perfection that ought to be there. Sin as such is essentially boring because it is the lack of something that could appeal to our wills and our minds.

What attracts men to evil acts is not the evil in them but the good that is there, seen under a false aspect and with a distorted perspective. The good seen from that angle is only the bait in a trap. When you reach out to take it, the trap is sprung and you are left with disgust, boredom—and hatred. Sinners are people who hate everything, because their world is necessarily full of betrayal, full of illusion, full of deception. And the greatest sinners are the most boring people in the world because they are also the most bored and the ones who find life most tedious.

When they try to cover the tedium of life by noise, excitement and violence—the inevitable fruits of a life devoted to the love of values that do not exist—they become something more than boring: they are scourges of the world and of society. And being scourged is not merely something dull or tedious.

Yet when it is all over and they are dead, the record of their sins in history becomes exceedingly uninteresting and is inflicted on school children as a penance which is all the more bitter because even an eight-year-old can readily see the uselessness of learning about people like Hitler, Stalin and Napoleon.

18

Faith

THE beginning of contemplation is faith. If there is something essentially sick about your conception of faith you will never be a contemplative.

First of all, faith is not an emotion, not a feeling. It is not a blind subconscious urge towards something vaguely supernatural. It is not simply an elemental need in man's spirit. It is not a feeling that God exists. It is not a conviction that one is somehow saved or "justified" for no special reason except that one happens to feel that way. It is not something entirely interior and subjective, with no reference to any external motive. It is not just "soul force." It is not something that bubbles up out of the recesses of your soul and fills you with an indefinable "sense" that everything is all right. It is not something so purely yours that its content is incommunicable. It is not some personal myth of your own that you cannot share with anyone else, and the objective validity of which does not matter either to you or God or anybody else.

But also it is not an opinion. It is not a conviction based on rational analysis. It is not the fruit of scientific evidence. You can only believe what you do not know. As soon as you know it, you no longer believe it, at least not in the same way as you know it.

Faith is first of all an intellectual assent. It perfects the mind, it does not destroy it. It puts the intellect in possession of Truth which reason cannot grasp by itself. It gives us certitude concerning God as He is in Himself; faith is the way to a vital contact with a God who is alive, and not to the view of an abstract First Principle worked out by syllogisms from the evidence of created things.

But the assent of faith is not based on the intrinsic evidence of a visible object. The act of belief unites two members of a proposition which have no connection in our natural experience. But also there is nothing within reach of reason to argue that they are disconnected. The statements which demand the assent of faith are simply neutral to reason. We have no natural evidence why they should be true or why they should be false. We assent to them because of something other than intrinsic evidence. We accept their truth as revealed and the motive of our assent is the authority of God who reveals them.

Faith is not expected to give complete satisfaction to the intellect. It leaves the intellect suspended in obscurity, without a light proper to its own mode of knowing. Yet it does not frustrate the intellect, or deny it, or destroy it. It pacifies it with a conviction which it knows it can accept quite rationally under the guidance of love. For the act of faith is an act in which the intellect is content to know God by *loving* Him and accepting His statements about Himself on His own terms. And this assent is quite rational because it is based on the realization that our reason can tell us nothing about God as He actually is in Himself, and on the fact that God Himself is infinite actuality and therefore infinite Truth, Wisdom, Power and Providence, and can reveal Himself with absolute certitude in any manner He pleases, and can certify His own revelation of Himself by external signs.

FAITH is primarily an intellectual assent. But if it were only that and nothing more, if it were only the "argument of what does not appear," it would not be complete. It has to be something more than an assent of the mind. It is also a grasp, a contact, a

communion of wills, "the substance of things to be hoped for."
By faith one not only assents to propositions revealed by God,
one not only attains to truth in a way that intelligence and
reason alone cannot do, but one assents to God Himself. One
receives God. One says "yes" not merely to a statement *about*
God, but to the Invisible, Infinite God Himself. One fully accepts
the statement not only for its own content, but for the sake of
Him who made it.

Too often our notion of faith is falsified by our emphasis on
the statements *about* God which faith believes, and by our
forgetfulness of the fact that faith is a communion with God's
own light and truth. Actually, the statements, the propositions
which faith accepts on the divine authority are simply media
through which one passes in order to reach the divine Truth.
Faith terminates not in a statement, not in a formula of words,
but in God.

If instead of resting in God by faith, we rest simply in the
proposition or the formula, it is small wonder that faith does
not lead to contemplation. On the contrary, it leads to anxious
hair-splitting arguments, to controversy, to perplexity and
ultimately to hatred and division.

It is of course quite true that theology can and must study the
intellectual content of revelation and especially the verbal
formulation of divinely revealed truth. But once again, this is
not the final object of faith. Faith goes beyond words and
formulas and brings us the light of God Himself.

The importance of the formulas is not that they are ends in
themselves, but that they are means through which God
communicates His truth to us. They must be kept clear.
They must be clean windows, so that they may not obscure
and hinder the light that comes to us. They must not falsify
God's truth. Therefore we must make every effort to believe
the right formulas. But we must not be so obsessed with

verbal correctness that we never go beyond the words to the
ineffable reality which they attempt to convey.

Faith, then, is not just the grim determination to cling to a
certain form of words, no matter what may happen—though
we must certainly be prepared to defend our creed with our life.
But above all, faith is the opening of an inward eye, the eye of
the heart, to be filled with the presence of divine light.

Ultimately faith is the only key to the universe. The final
meaning of human existence, and the answers to questions on
which all our happiness depends cannot be reached in any
other way.

19

From Faith to Wisdom

THE living God, the God who is God and not a philosopher's abstraction, lies infinitely beyond the reach of anything our eyes can see or our minds can understand. No matter what perfection you predicate of Him, you have to add that your concept is only a pale analogy of the perfection that is in God, and that He is not literally what you conceive by that term.

He who is infinite light is so tremendous in His evidence that our minds only see Him as darkness. *Lux in tenebris lucet et tenebrae eam non comprehenderunt.* (The Light shines in darkness and the darkness has not understood it.)

If nothing that can be seen can either be God or represent Him to us as He is, then to find God we must pass beyond everything that can be seen and enter into darkness. Since nothing that can be heard is God, to find Him we must enter into silence.

Since God cannot be imagined, anything our imagination tells us about Him is ultimately misleading and therefore we cannot know Him as He really is unless we pass beyond everything that can be imagined and enter into an obscurity without images and without the likeness of any created thing.

And since God cannot be seen or imagined, the visions of God we read of the saints having are not so much visions *of* Him as visions *about* Him; for to *see* any limited form is not to see Him.

GOD cannot be understood except by Himself. If we are to understand Him we can only do so by being in some way transformed into Him, so that we know Him as He knows Himself. And He does not know Himself by any representation of Himself: His own infinite Being is His own knowledge of Himself and we will not know Him as He knows Himself until we are united to what He is.

Faith is the first step in this transformation because it is a cognition that knows without images and representations by a loving identification with the living God in obscurity.

Faith reaches the intellect not simply through the senses but in a light directly infused by God. Since this light does not pass through the eye or the imagination or reason, its certitude becomes our own without any vesture of created appearance, without any likeness that can be visualized or described. It is true that the language of the article of faith to which we assent represents things that can be imagined, but in so far as we imagine them we misconceive them and tend to go astray. Ultimately we cannot imagine the connection between the two terms of the proposition: "In God there are Three Persons and One Nature." And it would be a great mistake to try.

If you believe, if you make a simple act of submission to the authority of God proposing some article of faith externally through His Church, you receive the gift of an interior light that is so simple that it baffles description and so pure that it would be coarse to call it an experience. But it is a true light, perfecting the intellect of man with a perfection far beyond knowledge.

It is of course necessary to remember that faith implies the acceptance of truths proposed by authority. But this element of submission in faith must not be so overemphasized that it seems to constitute the whole essence of faith: as if a mere unloving, unenlightened, dogged submission of the will to authority were enough to make a "man of faith." If this element of will is overemphasized then the difference between faith in the intellect and simple obedience in the will becomes obscured. In certain cases this can be very unhealthy, because actually if there is no *light* of faith, no interior illumination of the mind by grace by which one accepts the proposed truth *from God* and thereby attains to it, so to speak, in His divine assurance, then inevitably the mind lacks the true peace, the supernatural support which is due to it. In that event there is not real faith. The positive element of light is lacking. There is a forced suppression of doubt rather than the opening of the eye of the heart by deep belief. Where there is only a violent suppression of doubt and nothing more, can we suppose that the interior gift of faith has really been received? This is, of course, a very delicate question, because it often happens that where there is deep faith, accompanied by true consent of love to God and to His truth, there may yet persist difficulties in the imagination and in the intellect.

In a certain sense we may say that there are still "doubts," if by that we mean not that we hesitate to accept the truth of revealed doctrine, but that we feel the weakness and instability of our spirit in the presence of the awful mystery of God. This is not so much an objective doubt as a subjective sense of our own helplessness which is perfectly compatible with true faith. Indeed, as we grow in faith we also tend to grow in this sense of our own helplessness, so that a man who believes much may, at the same time, in this improper sense, seem to "doubt" more than ever before. This is no indication of theological doubt at all, but merely the perfectly normal awareness of natural insecurity and of the anguish that comes with it.

The very obscurity of faith is an argument of its perfection. It is darkness to our minds because it so far transcends their weakness. The more perfect faith is, the darker it becomes The closer we get to God, the less is our faith diluted with the half-light of created images and concepts. Our certainty increases with this obscurity, yet not without anguish and even material doubt, because we do not find it easy to subsist in a void in which our natural powers have nothing of their own to rely on. And it is in the deepest darkness that we most fully possess God on earth, because it is then that our minds are most truly liberated from the weak, created lights that are darkness in comparison to Him; it is then that we are filled with His infinite Light which seems pure darkness to our reason.

In this greatest perfection of faith the infinite God Himself becomes the Light of the darkened soul and possesses it entirely with His Truth. And at this inexplicable moment the deepest night becomes day and faith turns into understanding.

FROM all this it is evident that faith is not just one moment of the spiritual life, not just a step to something else. It is that acceptance of God which is the very climate of all spiritual living. It is the beginning of communion. As faith deepens, and as communion deepens with it, it becomes more and more intensive and at the same time reaches out to affect everything else we think and do. I do not mean merely that now all our thoughts are couched in certain fideist or pietistic formulas, but rather that faith gives a dimension of simplicity and *depth* to all our apprehensions and to all our experiences.

What is this dimension of depth? It is the incorporation of the unknown and of the unconscious into our daily life. Faith brings together the known and the unknown so that they overlap: or rather, so that we are *aware* of their overlapping. Actually, our whole life is a mystery of which very little comes to our conscious understanding. But when we *accept only what we can consciously rationalize*, our life is actually reduced to the most pitiful limitations, though we may think quite otherwise. (We have been brought up with the absurd prejudice that only what we can reduce to a rational and conscious formula is really understood and experienced in our life. When we can say *what* a thing is, or *what* we are doing, we think we fully grasp and experience it. In point of fact this verbalization— very often it is nothing more than verbalization—tends to cut us off from genuine experience and to obscure our understanding instead of increasing it.)

Faith does not simply *account for* the unknown, tag it with a theological tag and file it away in a safe place where we do not have to worry about it. This is a falsification of the whole idea of faith. On the contrary, faith incorporates the unknown into our everyday life in a living, dynamic and actual manner. The unknown remains unknown. It is still a mystery, for it cannot cease to be one. The function of faith is not to reduce mystery to rational clarity, but to integrate the unknown and the known together in a living whole, in which we are more and more able to transcend the limitations of our external self.

Hence the function of faith is not only to bring us into contact with the "authority of God" revealing; not only to teach us truths "about God," but even to reveal to us the unknown in our own selves, in so far as our unknown and undiscovered self actually lives in God, moving and acting only under the direct light of His merciful grace.

This is, to my mind, the crucially important aspect of faith which is too often ignored today. Faith is not just conformity, it is *life*. It embraces all the realms of life, penetrating into the most mysterious and inaccessible depths not only of our unknown spiritual being but even of God's own hidden essence and love. Faith, then, is the only way of opening up the true depths of reality, even of our own reality. Until a man yields himself to God in the consent of total belief, he must inevitably remain a stranger to himself, an exile from himself, because he is excluded from the most meaningful depths of his own being: those which remain obscure and unknown because they are too simple and too deep to be attained by reason.

At once the question arises: do you mean the subconscious mind? Here a distinction must be made. We tend to imagine ourselves as a conscious mind which is "above" and a subconscious mind that is "below the conscious." This image tends to be misleading. The conscious mind of man is *exceeded in all directions* by his unconscious. There is darkness not only below our conscious reason but also above it and all around it. Our conscious mind is by no means the summit of our being. Nor does it control all the rest of our being from a point of eminence. It merely controls some of the elements that are below it. But our conscious mind may in turn be controlled by the unconscious that is "beyond" it, whether above or below. However, it should not be controlled by what is below it, only by what is above. Hence the important distinction between the animal, emotional and instinctive components of our unconscious and the spiritual, one might almost say the "divine," elements in our superconscious mind.

Now faith actually brings *all* of the unconscious into integration with the rest of our life, but it does so in different ways. What is below us is accepted (not by any means merely rationalized). It is consented to in so far as it is willed by God. Faith enables us to come to terms with our animal nature and to accept the task of trying to govern it according to the divine will, that is, according to love. At the same time, faith subjects our reason to the hidden spiritual forces that are *above* it. In so doing, the whole man is brought into subjection to the "unknown" that is above him.

In this superconscious realm of mystery is hidden not only

the summit of man's spiritual being (which remains a pure mystery to his reason) but also the presence of God, who dwells at this hidden summit, according to traditional metaphor. Faith then brings man into contact with man's own inmost spiritual depths and with God, who is "present" within those same depths.

The traditional theology of the Greek Fathers devised three terms for these three aspects of man's one spirit. That which is unconscious and below reason was the *anima* or *psyche*, the "animal" soul, the realm of instinct and of emotion, the realm of automatism in which man functions as a psychophysical organism. This *anima* is conceived as a kind of feminine or passive principle in man.

Then there is the reason, the enlightened, conscious, active principle, the *animus* or *nous*. Here we have the mind as a masculine principle, the intelligence that governs, ratiocinates, guides our activity in the light of prudence and of thought. It is meant to direct and command the feminine principle, the passive *anima*. The *anima* is Eve, the *animus* is Adam. The effect of original sin in us all is that Eve tempts Adam and he yields his reasoned thought to her blind impulse, and tends henceforth to be governed by the automatism of passionate reaction, by conditioned reflex, rather than by thought and moral principle.

However, the true state of man is not just *anima* governed by *animus*, the masculine and the feminine. There is an even higher principle which is above the division of masculine and feminine, active and passive, prudential and instinctive. This higher principle in which both the others are joined and transcend themselves in union with God, is the *spiritus*, or *pneuma*. This higher principle is not merely something in man's nature, it is man himself united, vivified, raised above himself and inspired by God.

The full stature of man is to be found in "spirit" or *pneuma*. Man is not fully man until he is "one spirit" with God. Man is "spirit" when he is at once *anima*, *animus*, and *spiritus*. But these three are not numerically distinct. They are one. And when they are perfectly ordered in unity, while retaining their own rightful qualities, then man is reconstituted in the image of the Holy Trinity.

The "spiritual life" is then the perfectly balanced life in which the body with its passions and instincts, the mind with its reasoning and its obedience to principle and the spirit with its passive illumination by the Light and Love of God form one complete man who is in God and with God and from God and for God. One man in whom God is all in all. One man in whom God carries out His own will without obstacle.

It can easily be seen that a purely emotional worship, a life of instinct, an orgiastic religion, is no spiritual life. But also, a merely rational life, a life of conscious thought and rationally directed activity, is not a fully spiritual life. In particular it is a characteristic modern error to reduce a man's spirituality to mere "mentality," and to confine the whole spiritual life purely and simply in the reasoning mind. Then the spiritual life is reduced to a matter of "thinking"—of verbalizing, rationalizing, etc. But such a life is truncated and incomplete.

The true spiritual life is a life neither of dionysian orgy nor of apollonian clarity: it transcends both. It is a life of wisdom, a life of sophianic love. In *Sophia*, the highest wisdom-principle, all the greatness and majesty of the unknown that is in God and all that is rich and maternal in His creation are united inseparably, as paternal and maternal principles, the uncreated Father and created Mother-Wisdom.

Faith is what opens to us this higher realm of unity, of strength, of light, of sophianic love where there is no longer the limited and fragmentary light provided by rational principles, but where the Truth is One and Undivided and takes all to itself in the wholeness of *Sapientia*, or *Sophia*. When St. Paul said that Love was the fulfilment of the Law and that Love had delivered man from the Law, he meant that by the Spirit of Christ we were incorporated into Christ, Himself the "power and wisdom of God," so that Christ Himself thenceforth became our own life, and light and love and wisdom. Our full spiritual life is life in wisdom, life in Christ. The darkness of faith bears fruit in the light of wisdom.

A Simple Prayer

Lord, make me an instrument of your peace
Where there is hatred   let me sow love,
Where there is injury — — pardon,
Where there is doubt — — — faith,
Where there is despair — — hope,
Where there is darkness — light,
Where there is sadness — — joy.

O Divine Master, grant that I may not so much seek
To be consoled — — — as to console,
To be understood — — as to understand,
To be loved — — — — as to love,

for

It is in giving — — — that we receive,
It is in pardoning, that we are pardoned,
It is in dying — — that we are born to eternal life.

St. Francis.

PUBLISHED BY IONA COMMUNITY

20

Tradition and Revolution

THE biggest paradox about the Church is that she is at the same time essentially traditional and essentially revolutionary. But that is not as much of a paradox as it seems, because Christian tradition, unlike all others, is a living and perpetual revolution.

Human traditions all tend towards stagnation and decay. They try to perpetuate things that cannot be perpetuated. They cling to objects and values which time destroys without mercy. They are bound up with a contingent and material order of things—customs, fashions, styles and attitudes—which inevitably change and give way to something else.

The presence of a strong element of human conservatism in the Church should not obscure the fact that Christian tradition, supernatural in its source, is something absolutely opposed to human traditionalism.

The living tradition of Catholicism is like the breath of a physical body. It renews life by repelling stagnation. It is a constant, quiet, peaceful revolution against death.

As the physical act of breathing keeps the spiritual soul united to a material body whose very matter tends always to corrupt and decay, so Catholic tradition keeps the Church alive under the material and social and human elements which will be encrusted upon it as long as it is in the world.

The reason why Catholic tradition is a tradition is because there is only one living doctrine in Christianity. The whole truth of Christianity has been fully revealed: it has not yet been fully understood or fully lived. The life of the Church is the Truth of God Himself, breathed out into the Church by His Spirit, and there cannot be any other truth to supersede and replace it.

The only thing that can replace such intense life is a lesser life, a kind of death. The constant human tendency away from God and away from this living tradition can only be counter-acted by a return to tradition, a renewal and a deepening of the one unchanging life that was infused into the Church at the beginning.

And yet this tradition must always be a revolution because by its very nature it denies the values and standards to which human passion is so powerfully attached. To those who love money and pleasure and reputation and power this tradition says: "Be poor, go down into the far end of society, take the last place among men, live with those who are despised, love other men and serve them instead of making them serve you. Do not fight them when they push you around, but pray for those that hurt you. Do not look for pleasure, but turn away from things that satisfy your senses and your mind and look for God in hunger and thirst and darkness, through deserts of the spirit in which it seems to be madness to travel. Take upon yourself the burden of Christ's Cross, that is, Christ's humility and poverty and obedience and renunciation, and you will find peace for your souls."

This is the most complete revolution that has ever been preached; in fact, it is the only true revolution, because all the others demand the extermination of somebody else, but this one means the death of the man who, for all practical purposes, you have come to think of as your own self.

A REVOLUTION is supposed to be a change that turns everything completely around. But the ideology of political revolution will never change anything except appearances. There will be violence, and power will pass from one party to another, but when the smoke clears and the bodies of all the dead men are underground, the situation will be essentially the same as it was before: there will be a minority of strong men in power exploiting all the others for their own ends. There will be the same greed and cruelty and lust and ambition and avarice and hypocrisy as before.

For the revolutions of men change nothing. The only influence that can really upset the injustice and iniquity of men is the power that breathes in Christian tradition, renewing our participation in the Life that is the Light of men.

To those who have no personal experience of this revolutionary aspect of Christian truth, but who see only the outer crust of dead, human conservatism that tends to form around the Church the way barnacles gather on the hull of a ship, all this talk of dynamism sounds foolish.

Each individual Christian and each new age of the Church has to make this rediscovery, this return to the source of Christian life.

It demands a fundamental act of renunciation that accepts the necessity of starting out on the way to God under the guidance of other men. This acceptance can be paid for only by sacrifice, and ultimately only a gift of God can teach us the difference between the dry outer crust of formality which the Church sometimes acquires from the human natures that compose it, and the living inner current of divine Life which is the only real Catholic tradition.

THE notion of dogma terrifies men who do not understand the Church. They cannot conceive that a religious doctrine may be clothed in a clear, definite and authoritative statement without at once becoming static, rigid and inert and losing all its vitality. In their frantic anxiety to escape from any such conception they take refuge in a system of beliefs that is vague and fluid, a system in which truths pass like mists and waver and vary like shadows. They make their own personal selection of ghosts, in this pale, indefinite twilight of the mind. They take good care never to bring these abstractions out into the full brightness of the sun for fear of a full view of their unsubstantiality.

They favour the Catholic mystics with a sort of sympathetic regard, for they believe that these rare men somehow reached the summit of contemplation in defiance of Catholic dogma. Their deep union with God is supposed to have been an escape from the teaching authority of the Church, and an implicit protest against it.

But the truth is that the saints arrived at the deepest and most vital and also the most individual and personal knowledge of God precisely because of the Church's teaching authority, precisely through the tradition that is guarded and fostered by that authority.

The first step to contemplation is faith; and faith begins with an assent to Christ teaching through His Church; *fides ex auditu, qui vos audit, me audit.* "He that heareth you, heareth Me." And "faith cometh by hearing."

It is not the dry formula of a dogmatic definition by itself that pours light into the mind of a Catholic contemplative, but the assent to the content of that definition deepens and broadens into a vital, personal and incommunicable penetration of the supernatural truth which it expresses—an understanding that is a gift of the Holy Ghost and which merges into the Wisdom of Love, to possess Truth in its infinite Substance, God Himself.

The dogmas of Catholic faith are not merely symbols or vague rationalizations which we accept as arbitrary points of stimulation around which good moral actions may form or develop—still less is it true that any idea would serve just as well as those that have been defined, any old pious thought would foment this vague moral life in our souls. The dogmas defined and taught by the Church have a very precise, positive and definite meaning which those who have the grace to do so must explore and penetrate if they would live an integral spiritual life. For the understanding of dogma is the proximate and ordinary way to contemplation.

Everybody who can do so ought to acquire something of a theologian's accuracy and sharpness in appreciating the true sense of dogma. Every Christian ought to have as deep a comprehension of his belief as his state will allow him. And this means that every one ought to breathe the clean atmosphere of orthodox tradition and be able to explain his belief in correct terminology—and terminology with a content of genuine ideas.

Yet true contemplation is not arrived at by an effort of the mind. On the contrary, a man could easily lose his way in the forest of technical details which concern a professional theologian. But God gives true theologians a hunger born of humility, which cannot be satisfied with formulas and arguments, and which looks for something closer to God than analogy can bring you.

This serene hunger of the spirit penetrates the surface of words and goes beyond the human formulation of mysteries and seeks, in the humiliation of silence, intellectual solitude and interior poverty, the gift of a supernatural apprehension which words cannot truly signify.

Beyond the labour of argument it finds rest in faith and beneath the noise of discourse it apprehends the Truth, not in distinct and clear-cut definitions but in the limpid obscurity of a single intuition that unites all dogmas in one simple Light, shining into the soul directly from God's eternity, without the medium of created concept, without the intervention of symbols or of language or the likenesses of material things.

Here the Truth is One whom we not only know and possess but by whom we are known and possessed. Here theology ceases to be a body of abstractions and becomes a Living Reality who is God Himself. And He reveals Himself to us in our total gift of our lives to Him. Here the light of truth is not something that exists for our intellect but One in whom and for whom all minds and spirits exist, and theology does not truly begin to be theology until we have transcended the language and separate concepts of theologians.

That was why St. Thomas put the *Summa Theologica* aside in weariness before it was finished, saying that it was "all straw."

And yet when the contemplative returns from the depths of his simple experience of God and attempts to communicate it to men, he necessarily comes once again under the control of the theologian and his language is bound to strive after the clarity and distinctness and accuracy that canalize Catholic tradition.

Therefore beware of the contemplative who says that theology is all straw before he has ever bothered to read any.

21

The Mystery of Christ

AS a magnifying glass concentrates the rays of the sun into a little burning knot of heat that can set fire to a dry leaf or a piece of paper, so the mystery of Christ in the Gospel concentrates the rays of God's light and fire to a point that sets fire to the spirit of man. And this is why Christ was born and lived in the world and died and returned from death and ascended to His Father in heaven: *ut dum visibiliter Deum cognoscimus, per hunc in invisibilium amorem rapiamur.* Through the glass of His Incarnation He concentrates the rays of His divine Truth and Love upon us so that we feel the burn, and all mystical experience is communicated to men through the Man Christ.

For in Christ God is made Man. In Him God and man are no longer separate, remote from one another, but inseparably one, unconfused and yet indivisible. Hence in Christ everything that is divine and supernatural becomes accessible on the human level to every man born of woman, to every son of Adam. What is divine has now become connatural to us in Christ's love so that if we receive Him and are united with Him in friendship, He who is at the same time God and our brother, grants us the divine life that is now able to be ours on our human level. We become sons of God by adoption in so far as we are like Christ and His brothers.

God is everywhere. His truth and His love pervade all things as the light and the heat of the sun pervade our atmosphere. But just as the rays of the sun do not set fire to anything by themselves, so God does not touch our souls with the fire of supernatural knowledge and experience without Christ.

But the glass of that Manhood seeks out spirits that are well prepared, dried by the light and warmth of God, and ready to take flame in the little knot of fire that is the grace of the Holy Ghost.

The normal way to contemplation is a belief in Christ that is born of thoughtful consideration of His life and His teaching. But just because all experience of God comes to us through Christ, that does not necessarily mean that every contemplative always, invariably, arrives at his contemplation through Christ as He may exist in our *imagination*. For the imagination is only one of the means for keeping the object of our belief before our minds. We do not always have to force ourselves to picture Christ as we think He must have looked, or ought to have looked, for really no one can be quite sure just *how* He looked.

Spiritual writers in the past have made rather a problem of this, although it is hard to see why there should be any problem at all. Faith in Christ, and in the mysteries of His life and death, is the foundation of the Christian life and the source of all contemplation: and about this there can be no issue. No one can dismiss the Man Christ from his interior life on the pretext that he has now entered by higher contemplation into direct communication with the Word. For the Man Christ *is* the Word of God, even though His human nature is not His divine nature. The two are united in One Person and are One Person, so that the Man Christ is God.

THE supposed "problem" as to whether in contemplation one should abandon the humanity of Christ in order to go directly to His divinity arises from a too superficial grasp of dogma. And this is one of the cases where ignorance of theology has disastrous effects in the interior life. Not that one is expected to understand clearly the hypostatic union, in order to be a contemplative. But if one is going to introduce dogmatic formulas into his explication of interior experience, these formulas had better be correct ones, otherwise the experience itself will be falsified and become illusory.

The Nestorian heresy arose from an inability to conceive two natures, the divine and the human, in Christ otherwise than as two separately subsisting beings. Hence Christ is not One Person who is divine and human, thinks the Nestorian, but He is *two beings*, God and "a man united to God."

If in our contemplation we so separate the humanity and divinity of Christ that we "pass beyond the humanity," to "rest in the divinity," we will tend to divide Christ into "A Man" and "A Divine Person," whereas in actuality God and man in Him are completely indivisible and inseparable in the Unity of His Person.

The weakness of Nestorianism is that it equates the nature with the person. But Christian contemplation is supremely personalistic. Our love and knowledge of Christ do not terminate in His human *nature* or in His divine *nature* but in His *Person*. To love Him merely as a *nature* would be like loving a human friend for his money or his conviviality. We do not love Christ for what He has but for *Who He is*.

The "what" in Christ is vastly less important than the "Who." The "what" may or may not be imaginable, but we reach the "Who"—the mysterious ineffable Divine Person— *directly and immediately* through grace and love, without images (or *with* them if you like, but this is less direct) and without rationalization. The real mystery of Christian *agapé* (charity) is this power that the Person of the Word, in coming to us, has given to us. The power of a direct and simple contact with Him, not as with an *object* only, a "thing" seen or imagined, but in the trans-subjective union of love which does

E

not unite an object with a subject but *two subjects in one affective union*. Hence, in love we can, so to speak, experience in our own hearts the intimate personal secret of the Beloved. And Christ has granted us His Friendship so that He may in this manner enter our hearts and dwell in them as a personal presence, not as an *object*, not as a "what" but as a "Who." Thus He Who is, is present in the depths of our own being as our Friend, and as our other self. Such is the mystery of the Word dwelling in us by virtue of His Incarnation and our incorporation in His Mystical Body, the Church.

This personal presence of Christ the Word in our souls is what I spoke of above as His "Mission."

IT is faith and not imagination that gives us supernatural life, faith that justifies us, faith that leads us to contemplation. "My just man liveth by faith," not imagination. Imagination only enters into it accidentally. If you need to use your imagination in order to remind yourself of the Christ in whom you believe, go ahead and use it. But if you can exercise your faith in Him without the bother of always conjuring up some picture of Him, so much the better: your faith will be simpler and purer.

FOR some people it is quite easy to turn within themselves and find a picture of Christ in their imagination, and this is an easy beginning of prayer. But for others this does not succeed. On the contrary, the effort it costs may fill their heads with problems and disturbances that make prayer impossible. Yet at the same time the mere name of Jesus or the indistinct, unanalysed notion of Christ is enough to keep their faith fully occupied in a simple and loving awareness of Him who is really present in our souls by the gift of His Personal love and by His divine Mission.

This loving awareness is a thing more real and more valuable than anything we can arrive at by our interior senses alone, for the picture of Jesus we may have in our imagination remains nothing but a picture, while the love that His grace produces in our hearts can bring us into direct contact with Him as He really is. For Jesus Himself causes this love to spring up within us, by a direct and personal effect of His will. When He touches our souls with His love, He affects us even more directly and intimately than a material object moves and affects our eyes or our other senses. Besides, the only real reason why we meditate on Jesus and reflect on the images of Him in our memory is in order that we may be prepared for this more intimate contact with Him by love. Therefore, when His love begins to burn within us, there is surely no strict necessity for using our imaginations any more. Some may like to, some may not, and others have no choice, one way or another. Use whatever helps you, and avoid what gets in your way.

EVERY one of us forms an idea of Christ that is limited and incomplete. It is cut according to our own measure. We tend to create for ourselves a Christ in our own image, a projection of our own aspirations, desires and ideals. We find in Him what we want to find. We make Him not only the incarnation of God but also the incarnation of the things we and our society and our part of society happen to live for.

Therefore, although it is true that perfection consists in imitating Christ and reproducing Him in our own lives, it is not enough merely to imitate the Christ we have in our imaginations.

We read the Gospels not merely to get a picture or an idea of Christ but to enter in and pass through the words of revelation to establish, by faith, a vital contact with the Christ who dwells in our souls as God.

The problem of forming Christ in us is not to be solved

merely by our own efforts. It is not a matter of studying the Gospels and then working to put our ideas into practice, although we should try to do that too, but always under the guidance of grace, in complete subjection to the Holy Spirit.

For if we depend on our own ideas, our own judgment and our own efforts to reproduce the life of Christ, we will only act out some kind of pious charade which will ultimately scare everybody we meet because it will be so stiff and artificial and so dead.

It is the Spirit of God that must teach us who Christ is and form Christ in us and transform us into other Christs. After all, transformation into Christ is not just an individual affair: there is only one Christ, not many. He is not divided. And for me to become Christ is to enter into the Life of the Whole Christ, the Mystical Body made up of the Head and the members, Christ and all who are incorporated in Him by His Spirit.

Christ forms Himself by grace and faith in the souls of all who love Him, and at the same time He draws them all together in Himself to make them One in Him. *Ut sint consummati in unum.*

And the Holy Ghost, who is the life of this One Body, dwells in the whole Body and in every one of the members so that the whole Christ is Christ and each individual is Christ.

THEREFORE if you want to have in your heart the affections and dispositions that were those of Christ on earth, consult not your own imagination but faith. Enter into the darkness of interior renunciation, strip your soul of images and let Christ form Himself in you by His Cross.

22

Life in Christ

TO live "in Christ" is to live in a mystery equal to that of the Incarnation and similar to it. For as Christ unites in His one Person the two natures of God and of man, so too in making us His friends He dwells in us, uniting us intimately to Himself. Dwelling in us He becomes as it were our superior self, for He has united and identified our inmost self with Himself. From the moment that we have responded by faith and charity to His love for us, a supernatural union of our souls with His indwelling Divine Person gives us a participation in His divine sonship and nature. A "new being" is brought into existence. I become a "new man" and this new man, spiritually and mystically one identity, is at once Christ and myself. The language of the New Testament and the teaching of the Church explain, to the mind of the believer, that this spiritual union of my being with Christ in one "new man" is the work of the Holy Spirit, the Spirit of Love, the Spirit of Christ.

The union of the two natures in the one Person of the Word, in Christ, is a union that is ontologically perfect and indestructible, a union of essences in one subsisting Personal entity who is the Eternal God. The union of my soul with God in Christ is not of this ontological or inseparable character. It is, on the contrary, an accidental union: yet it is more than just a moral union or an agreement of hearts. The union of the Christian with Christ is not just a similarity of inclination and feeling, a mutual consent of minds and wills. It has a more radical, more mysterious and supernatural quality: it is a

mystical union in which Christ Himself becomes the source
and principle of divine life in me. Christ Himself, to use a
metaphor based on Scripture, "breathes" in me divinely in
giving me His Spirit. The ever renewed mission of the Spirit
to the soul that is in the grace of Christ is to be understood by
the analogy of the natural breath that keeps renewing, from
moment to moment, our bodily life. The mystery of the
Spirit is the mystery of selfless love. We receive Him in the
"inspiration" of secret love, and we give Him to others in the
outgoing of our own charity. Our life in Christ is then a life
both of receiving and of giving. We receive from God, in the
Spirit, and in the same Spirit we return our love to God through
our brothers.

IF I have this divine life in me, what do the accidents of pain
and pleasure, hope and fear, joy and sorrow matter to me?
They are not my life and they have little to do with it. Why
should I fear anything that cannot rob me of God, and why
should I desire anything that cannot give me possession of Him?

Exterior things come and go, but why should they disturb
me? Why should joy excite me or sorrow cast me down,
achievement delight me or failure depress me, life attract or
death repel me if I live only in the Life that is within me by God's
gift?

Why should I worry about losing a bodily life that I must
inevitably lose anyway, as long as I possess a spiritual life and
identity that cannot be lost against my desire? Why should I
fear to cease to be what I am not when I have already become
something of what I am? Why should I go to great labour to
possess satisfactions that cannot last an hour, and which bring
misery after them, when I already own God in His eternity of
joy?

It is the easiest thing in the world to possess this life and this joy; all you have to do is believe and love; and yet people waste their whole lives in appalling labour and difficulty and sacrifice to get things that make real life impossible.

This is one of the chief contradictions that sin has brought into our souls: we have to do violence to ourselves to keep from labouring uselessly for what is bitter and without joy, and we have to compel ourselves to take what is easy and full of happiness as though it were against our interests, because for us the line of least resistance leads in the way of greatest hardship, and sometimes for us to do what is, in itself, most easy can be the hardest thing in the world.

Souls are like wax waiting for a seal. By themselves they have no special identity. Their destiny is to be softened and prepared in this life, by God's will, to receive, at their death, the seal of their own degree of likeness to God in Christ.

And this is what it means, among other things, to be judged by Christ.

The wax that has melted in God's will can easily receive the stamp of its identity, the truth of what it was meant to be. But the wax that is hard and dry and brittle and without love will not take the seal: for the hard seal, descending upon it, grinds it to powder.

Therefore if you spend your life trying to escape from the heat of the fire that is meant to soften and prepare you to become your true self, and if you try to keep your substance from melting in the fire—as if your true identity were to be hard wax—the seal will fall upon you at last and crush you. You will not be able to take your own true name and countenance, and you will be destroyed by the event that was meant to be your fulfilment.

A CONTEMPLATIVE priest will have a deep and absorbing sense

of union with Christ as priest and as offering in the Eucharistic sacrifice—so much so that his Mass will be going on within him not only when he is at the altar but when he is away from it, and at many different moments during the day.

I write this without being yet a priest, because I have known it to some degree merely by kneeling by the altar as server. The broken Host lies on the paten. But the fact that you are in possession of the secret identifies you with the Saviour and with what is going on. And without words or explicit acts of thought you make assent to this within yourself simply by staying where you are and looking on.

There Christ develops your life into Himself like a photograph.

Then a continual Mass, a deep and urgent sense of identification with an act of incomprehensible scope and magnitude that somehow has its focus in the centre of your own soul, pursues you wherever you go; and in all situations of your daily life it makes upon you secret and insistent demands for agreement and consent.

This truth is so tremendous that it is somehow neutral. It cannot be expressed. It is entirely personal. And you have no special desire to tell anybody about it. It is nobody else's business.

Not even distracting duties and work will be able to interfere with it altogether. You keep finding this anonymous Accomplice burning within you like a deep and peaceful fire.

Perhaps you will not be able completely to identify this presence and this continuous action going on within you unless it happens to be taking place formally on the altar before you: but at least then, obscurely, you will recognize in the breaking of the Bread the Stranger who was your companion yesterday and the day before. And like the disciples of Emmaus, you will realize how fitting it was that your heart should burn within you when the incidents of your day's work spoke to you of the Christ who lived and worked and offered His sacrifice within you all the time.

LIFE in Christ is life in the mystery of the Cross. It is not only a hidden supernatural participation in the divine life in eternity, but a participation in a divine mystery, a *sacred action* in which God Himself enters into time and, with the co-operation of men who have answered His call and have been united in a holy assembly, the Church, carries out the work of man's redemption.

We have to a great extent lost the sense of sacrifice. Today, where the notion of sacrifice is remembered at all, it seems to retain only a small portion of its true meaning. Popularly, even among Christians, a sacrifice is regarded only as a moral act, a work of piety or of virtue, which is marked by a special difficulty. It is then a "good deed" which is also hard and which "costs us something." The implication seems to be that sacrifice is something *subjective* and *hard*.

The true notion of sacrifice is, on the contrary, something quite objective and the note of difficulty or pain is not essential to it except in so far as our weak and fallen nature comes into conflict with the divine will. By rights, there is no reason why a perfect sacrifice should not also be painless: a pure act of adoration, a hymn to the divine glory sung in ecstatic peace.

A sacrifice is an action which is *objectively sacred*, primarily of a *social* character, and what is important is not so much the pain or difficulty attached to it as the *meaning*, the *sacred significance* which not only conveys an idea but *effects a divine and religious transformation* in the worshipper, thus consecrating and uniting him more closely to God.

The mystery of the Cross, of the redemptive death and resurrection of the Saviour, is renewed each day in the

Eucharistic sacrifice, popularly known as "the Mass." Here we have an action which is objectively sacred if ever there was one: the sacrificial action by which the Son of God offered Himself as a victim for the sins of man, on the Cross. This action is really, though mystically, represented by the Church, through her ordained priests, assisted by other ministers and by the faithful. Generally speaking there is nothing about the Mass to cause suffering either to the priest, to the ministers or to anyone present. Accidentally, of course, someone may have to get up unusually early in the morning, or travel for a long distance, or negotiate some other obstacle in order to assist at Mass: this subjective difficulty is certainly an occasion for a purer spiritual participation in the sacrifice, but it remains something exterior and accidental to it.

Every Mass has a social character, even though only the server may be assisting at it. Ideally speaking, the social nature of the Mass should be brought out by the active liturgical participation of all the faithful who are present, and the normal form of this participation is a sung Mass in which the faithful themselves sing and understand notable portions of the liturgy, and listen attentively to what is said or sung by the choir and the sacred ministers. Communion is the normal fullness of participation in the sacrifice.

The Christian who attends Mass intelligently is then participating in a sacred, objective, social act in which Christ is invisibly present as the chief worshipper, the High Priest, represented by His visible minister at the altar. Also, however, and in an even more intimate and mysterious presence, the Body and Blood of Christ are really present and are offered by the priest for the faithful in a state of immolation symbolized by the consecration of the separate species of bread and wine.

The liturgical sacrifice of the Church has at once a mystical and a cosmic significance. The communion of the faithful in

the Body and Blood of the Saviour not only really joins them
to Him in a sacramentally mystical union but also unites them
to one another in Christian charity and in the Holy Spirit.
In signifying this union, the sacrifice also produces, by Christ's
grace, what it signifies.

The cosmic aspect of the sacrifice is suggested by the very
nature of the gifts offered to God. Bread and wine, the produce
of the earth and of man's toil, are transformed into the Body
and Blood of Christ. Thus the whole creation as well as the
labour of man in all his legitimate natural aspirations are in
some way elevated, consecrated and transformed. The whole
world enters into a hymn of glory in honour of the Creator and
Saviour. This is the perfect sacrifice.

23

The Woman Clothed with the Sun

ALL that has been written about the Virgin Mother of God proves to me that hers is the most hidden of sanctities. What people find to say about her sometimes tells us more about their own selves than it does about Our Lady. For since God has revealed very little to us about her, men who know nothing of who and what she was tend to reveal themselves when they try to add something to what God has told us about her.

And the things we do know about her only make the true character and quality of her sanctity seem more hidden. We believe that hers was the perfect sanctity outside the sanctity of Christ her Son, who is God. But the sanctity of God is only darkness to our minds. Yet the sanctity of the Blessed Virgin is in a way more hidden than the sanctity of God: because He has at least told us something about Himself that is objectively valid when it is put into human language. But about Our Lady He has told us only a few important things— and even then we cannot grasp the fullness of what they mean. For all He has told us about her soul amounts to this: that it was absolutely full of the most perfect created holiness. But what that means, in detail, we have no sure way of knowing. Therefore the other certain thing we know about her is that her sanctity is most hidden.

And yet I can find her if I too become hidden in God where

she is hidden. To share her humility and hiddenness and poverty, her concealment and solitude is the best way to know her: but to know her thus is to find wisdom. *Qui me inveniet vitam et haurie satlutem a Domino.*

IN the actual living, human person who is the Virgin Mother of Christ are all the poverty and all the wisdom of all the saints. It all came to them through her, and is in her. The sanctity of all the saints is a participation in her sanctity, because in the order He has established God wills that all graces come to men through Mary.

That is why to love her and to know her is to discover the true meaning of everything and to have access to all wisdom. Without her, the knowledge of Christ is only speculation. But in her it becomes experience because all the humility and poverty, without which Christ cannot be known, were given to her. Her sanctity is the silence in which alone Christ can be heard, and the voice of God becomes an experience to us through her contemplation.

The emptiness and interior solitude and peace without which we cannot be filled with God were given by Him to Mary in order that she might receive Him into the world by offering Him the hospitality of a being that was perfectly pure, perfectly silent, perfectly at rest, perfectly at peace, and centred in utter humility. If we ever manage to empty ourselves of the noise of the world and of our own passions, it is because she has been sent close to us by God and given us a share in her sanctity and her hiddenness.

MARY alone, of all the saints, is, in everything, incomparable. She has the sanctity of them all and yet resembles none of them. And still we can talk of being like her. This likeness to her is not only something to desire—it is one human quality most worthy of our desire: but the reason for that is that she, of all creatures, most perfectly recovered the likeness to God that God willed to find, in varying degrees, in us all.

It is necessary, no doubt, to talk about her privileges as if they were something that could be made comprehensible in human language and could be measured by some human standard. It is most fitting to talk about her as a Queen and to act as if you knew what it meant to say she has a throne above all the angels. But this should not make anyone forget that her highest privilege is her poverty and her greatest glory is that she is most hidden, and the source of all her power is that she is as nothing in the presence of Christ, of God.

This is often forgotten by Catholics themselves, and therefore it is not surprising that those who are not Catholics often have a completely wrong conception of Catholic devotion to the Mother of God. They imagine, and sometimes we can understand their reasons for doing so, that Catholics treat the Blessed Virgin as an almost divine being in her own right, as if she had some glory, some power, some majesty of her own that placed her on a level with Christ Himself. They regard the Assumption of Mary into heaven as a kind of apotheosis and her Queenship as a strict divinization. Hence her place in the Redemption would seem to be equal to that of her Son. But this is all completely contrary to the true mind of the Catholic Church. It forgets that Mary's chief glory is in her nothingness, in the fact of being the "*Handmaid* of the Lord," as one who in becoming the Mother of God acted simply in loving submission to His command, in the pure obedience of faith. She is blessed not because of some mythical pseudo-divine prerogative, but in all her human and womanly limitations as *one who has believed*. It is the faith and the fidelity of this humble handmaid, "full of grace," that enables her to be the perfect instrument of God, and nothing else but His instrument. The work that was done in her was purely the work of God. "He that is mighty hath done great things in me." The glory of Mary is purely and simply the glory of God in her, and she, like anyone else, can say that she has nothing that she has not received from Him through Christ.

As a matter of fact, this is precisely her greatest glory: that having nothing of her own, retaining nothing of a "self" that could glory in anything for her own sake, she placed no obstacle to the mercy of God and in no way resisted His love and His will. Hence she received *more* from Him than any other saint. He was able to accomplish His will perfectly in her, and His liberty was in no way hindered or turned from its purpose by the presence of an egotistical self in Mary. She was and is in the highest sense a person precisely because, being "immaculate," she was free from every taint of selfishness that might obscure God's light in her being. She was then a freedom that obeyed Him perfectly and in this obedience found the fulfilment of perfect love.

THE genuine significance of Catholic devotion to Mary is to be seen in the light of the Incarnation itself. The Church cannot separate the Son and the Mother. Because the Church conceives of the Incarnation as God's descent into flesh and into time, and His great gift of Himself to His creatures, she also believes that the one who was closest to Him in this great mystery was the one who participated most perfectly in the gift. When a room is heated by an open fire, surely there is nothing strange in the fact that those who stand closest to the fireplace are the ones who are warmest. And when God comes into the world through the instrumentality of one of His servants, then there is nothing surprising about the fact that His chosen instrument should have the greatest and most intimate share in the divine gift.

Mary, who was empty of all egotism, free from all sin, was as pure as the glass of a very clean window that has no other function than to admit the light of the sun. If we rejoice in that light, we implicitly praise the cleanness of the window. And of course it might be argued that in such a case we might well forget the window altogether. This is true. And yet the Son of God, in emptying Himself of His majestic power, having become a child, abandoning Himself in complete dependence to the loving care of a human mother, in a certain sense draws our attention once again to her. The Light has wished to remind us of the window, because He is grateful to her and because He has an infinitely tender and personal love for her. If He asks us to share this love, it is certainly a great grace and a privilege, and one of the most important aspects of this privilege is that it enables us to some extent to appreciate the mystery of God's great love and respect for His creatures.

THAT God should assume Mary into heaven is not just a glorification of a "Mother Goddess." Quite the contrary, it is the expression of the divine love for humanity, and a very special manifestation of God's respect for His creatures, His desire to do honour to the beings He has made in His own image, and most particularly His respect for the *body* which was destined to be the temple of His glory. If Mary is believed to be assumed into heaven, it is because we too are one day, by the grace of God, to dwell where she is. If human nature is glorified in her, it is because God desires it to be glorified in us too, and it is for this reason that His Son, taking flesh, came into the world.

In all the great mystery of Mary, then, one thing remains most clear: that of herself she is nothing, and that God has for our sakes delighted to manifest His glory and His love in her.

It is because she is, of all the saints, the most perfectly poor and most perfectly hidden, the one who has absolutely nothing whatever that she attempts to possess as her own, that she can most fully communicate to the rest of us the grace of the infinitely selfless God. And we will most truly possess Him when we have emptied ourselves and become poor and hidden as she is, resembling Him by resembling her.

And all our sanctity depends on her maternal love. The ones she desires to share the joy of her own poverty and simplicity, the ones whom she wills to be hidden as she is hidden, are the ones who share her closeness to God.

IT is a tremendous grace, then, and a great privilege when a person living in the world we have to live in suddenly loses his interest in the things that absorb that world, and discovers in his own soul an appetite for poverty and solitude. And the most precious of all the gifts of nature or grace is the desire to be hidden and to vanish from the sight of men and be accounted as nothing by the world and to disappear from one's own self-conscious consideration and vanish into nothingness in the immense poverty that is the adoration of God.

This absolute emptiness, this poverty, this obscurity holds within it the secret of all joy because it is full of God. To seek this emptiness is true devotion to the Mother of God. To find it is to find her. And to be hidden in its depths is to be full of God as she is full of Him, and to share her mission of bringing Him to all men.

Yet all generations must call her blessed, because they all receive through her obedience whatever supernatural life and joy is granted to them. And it is necessary that the world should acknowledge her and that the praise of God's great work in her should be sung in poetry and that cathedrals should be built in her name. For unless Our Lady is recognized as the Mother of God and as the Queen of all the saints and angels and as the hope of the world, faith in God will remain incomplete. How can we ask Him for all the things He would have us hope for if we do not know, by contemplating the sanctity of the Immaculate Virgin, what great things He has power to accomplish in the souls of men?

And so, the more we are hidden in the depths where her secret is discovered, the more we will want to praise her name in the world and glorify, in her, the God who made her His shining tabernacle. Yet we will not altogether trust our own talent to find words in which to praise her: for even if we could sing of her as did Dante or St. Bernard we would still have little to say of her, compared with the Church who alone knows how to praise her adequately and who dares to apply to her the inspired words God uses of His own Wisdom. Thus we find her living in the midst of Scripture, and unless we find her, also, hidden in Scripture wherever and in whatever promises contain her Son, we shall not fully know the life that is in Scripture.

It is she who, in these last days, is destined by the merciful delegation of God to manifest the power He has given to her because of her poverty, and save the last men living in the ruins of the burnt world. But if the world's last age, by the wickedness of men, is likely to be made the most terrible, yet by the clemency of the Blessed Virgin will it also be, for the poor who have received His mercy, the most victorious and the most joyful.

24

He who is not with Me
is against Me

A MAN who has been killed by one enemy is just as dead as one who has been killed by a whole army. If you are friends with one habit of mortal sin you live in death, even though you may seem to have all the other virtues.

SOME people think it is enough to have one virtue, like kindness or broadmindedness or charity, and let everything else go. But if you are unselfish in one way and selfish in twenty-five other ways your virtue will not do you much good. In fact, it will probably turn out to be nothing more than a twenty-sixth variety of the same selfishness, disguised as virtue.

Therefore do not think that because you seem to have some good quality, all the evil in you can be excused or forgotten on that account alone.

Do not think that you can show your love for Christ by hating those who seem to be His enemies on earth. Suppose they really do hate Him: nevertheless He loves them, and you cannot be united with Him unless you love them too.

If you hate the enemies of the Church instead of loving them, you too will run the risk of becoming an enemy of the Church, and of Christ; for He said: "Love your enemies," and He also said: "He who is not with me is against me." Therefore if you do not side with Christ by loving those that He loves, you are against Him.

But Christ loves all men. Christ died for all men. And Christ said there was no greater love than that a man should lay down his life for his friend.

Do not be too quick to assume your enemy is a savage just because he is *your* enemy. Perhaps he is your enemy because he thinks you are a savage. Or perhaps he is afraid of you because he feels that you are afraid of him. And perhaps if he believed you were capable of loving him he would no longer be your enemy.

Do not be too quick to assume that your enemy is an enemy of God just because he is *your* enemy. Perhaps he is your enemy precisely because he can find nothing in you that gives glory to God. Perhaps he fears you because he can find nothing in you of God's love and God's kindness and God's patience and mercy and understanding of the weaknesses of men.

Do not be too quick to condemn the man who no longer believes in God, for it is perhaps your own coldness and avarice, your mediocrity and materialism, your sensuality and selfishness that have killed his faith.

A MAN cannot be a perfect Christian—that is, a saint—unless he is also a communist. This means that he must either absolutely give up all right to possess anything at all, or else only use what he himself needs, of the goods that belong to him, and administer the rest for other men and for the poor: and in his determination of what he needs he must be governed to a great extent by the gravity of the needs of others.

But you will say it is practically impossible for a rich man to put into practice this clear teaching of Scripture and Catholic tradition. You are right. And there is nothing new in that. Christ told everybody the same thing long ago when He said it was easier for a camel to get through the eye of a needle than it was for a rich man to enter the Kingdom of Heaven.

If Christians had lived up to the Church's teaching about property and poverty there would never have been any occasion for the spurious communism of the Marxists and all the rest—whose communism starts out by denying *other men* the right to own property.

There is only one true doctrine about property rights, and that is taught by Catholic tradition. Those rights exist and cannot be denied, but they imply an obligation which, if it were put into practice without hypocrisy, self-deception and subterfuge, would mean that most Christians would be living with something like the communism of the first Apostles: "For neither was there any needy among them. For as many as were owners of lands or houses sold them and brought the price of the things they sold, and laid it down before the feet of the apostles. And distribution was made to every one according as he had need."

No one denied those men the right to own land, or to keep what they owned, or to sell it and give away their money. Yet that right implied an obligation to satisfy the needs of others as well as their own, and brought with it the privilege of doing so in a manner that was beyond the strict letter of any law and which could go as far as a charity that was heroic.

If you have money, consider that perhaps the only reason God allowed it to fall into your hands was in order that you might find joy and perfection by giving it all away.

It is easy enough to tell the poor to accept their poverty as God's will when you yourself have warm clothes and plenty of food and medical care and a roof over your head and no worry about the rent. But if you want them to believe you— try to share some of their poverty and see if you can accept it as God's will yourself!

25

Humility against Despair

DESPAIR is the absolute extreme of self-love. It is reached when a man deliberately turns his back on all help from anyone else in order to taste the rotten luxury of knowing himself to be lost.

In every man there is hidden some root of despair because in every man there is pride that vegetates and springs weeds and rank flowers of self-pity as soon as our own resources fail us. But because our own resources inevitably fail us, we are all more or less subject to discouragement and to despair.

Despair is the ultimate development of a pride so great and so stiff-necked that it selects the absolute misery of damnation rather than accept happiness from the hands of God and thereby acknowledge that He is above us and that we are not capable of fulfilling our destiny by ourselves.

But a man who is truly humble cannot despair, because in the humble man there is no longer any such thing as self-pity.

IT is almost impossible to overestimate the value of true humility and its power in the spiritual life. For the beginning of humility is the beginning of blessedness and the consummation of humility is the perfection of all joy. Humility contains in itself the answer to all the great problems of the life of the soul. It is the only key to faith, with which the spiritual life begins: for faith and humility are inseparable. In perfect humility all selfishness disappears and your soul no longer lives for itself: and it is lost and submerged in God and trans-formed into Him.

At this point of the spiritual life humility meets the highest exaltation of greatness. It is here that every one who humbles himself is exalted because, living no longer for himself or on the human level, the spirit is delivered of all the limitations and vicissitudes of creaturehood and of contingency, and swims in the attributes of God, whose power, magnificence, greatness and eternity have, through love, through humility, become our own.

If we were incapable of humility we would be incapable of joy, because humility alone can destroy the self-centredness that makes joy impossible.

IF there were no humility in the world, everybody would long ago have committed suicide.

THERE is a false humility which thinks it is pride to desire the highest greatness—the perfection of contemplation, the sum-mit of mystical union with God. This is one of the biggest illusions in the spiritual life because it is only in this greatness, only in this exalted union, that we can achieve perfect humility.

Yet it is easy to see how this mistake is made: and, in fact, from a certain point of view it is not a mistake at all. For if we consider the joy of mystical union abstractly, merely as some-thing which perfects our own being and gives us the highest possible happiness and satisfaction, it is possible to desire it with a desire that is selfish and full of pride. This pride will be all the greater if our desire implies that this consummation is somehow due to us, as if we had a right to it, as if there were something we could do to earn it for ourselves.

This is the way mystical union appears in the minds of those who do not realize that the essence of that union is a pure and selfless love that empties the soul of all pride and annihilates it in the sight of God, so that nothing may be left of it but the pure capacity for Him.

The joy of the mystical love of God springs from a liberation from all self-hood by the annihilation of every trace of pride. Desire not to be exalted but only to be abased, not to be great but only little in your own eyes and the eyes of the world: for the only way to enter into that joy is to dwindle down to a vanishing point and become absorbed in God through the centre of your own nothingness. The only way to possess His greatness is to pass through the needle's eye of your own absolute insufficiency.

The perfection of humility is found in transforming union. Only God can bring you to that purity through the fires of interior trial. It would be foolish not to desire such perfection. For what would be the good of being humble in a way that prevented you from seeking the consummation of all humility?

THOUGH it is intrinsically reasonable and right to desire mystical union with God, we so easily misunderstand what this means that it can sometimes become the most dangerous of all desires. To desire God is the most fundamental of all human desires. It is the very root of all our quest for happiness. Even the sinner, who seeks happiness where it cannot be found, is following a blind, errant desire for God which is not aware of itself. So that, from one point of view, it is impossible not to desire God.

On the other hand, when you use the expression to "desire God" you implicitly reduce God to the status of an "object" or of a "thing," as if He were "something" that could be grasped and possessed the way we possess riches, or knowledge, or some other created entity. And though it is true that we are bound to hope for the fulfilment of our deepest needs in the vision of God, yet it is at the same time very dangerous to think of God merely as the satisfaction of all our needs and desires. In so doing, we tend inevitably to distort and even to desecrate His holy and infinite truth.

I have seen many men enter monasteries with an earnest, devouring hunger for God, for contemplative experience. And I have seen them leave the monastery beaten and frustrated by the very intensity of their unfulfilled desires. There is no hope more cruel than the vain hope for a supreme fulfilment that is so misunderstood as to be utterly impossible. There is no defeat more terrible than the defeat of the human heart driven wild by its desire of a mystical mirage.

What makes this defeat so cruel is the inexorable complacency of the teachers of the spiritual life who insist that "if you have not found God it is because you have refused Him something. You have not consented to pay the price." As if union with God were something put up for sale in monasteries like ham or cheese, a kind of secret bargain offered to men on the contemplative black market—offered to this or that unfortunate buyer at the precise moment when his pockets were empty.

Did not Isaias say clearly that the waters of life are given to those, precisely, who have no money?

It is the duty of anyone who has had even the faintest glimpse of God's love to protest against an inhumanly cruel and false psychology of mysticism, this psychology which presents "sanctity" and "contemplation" under the guise of riches to be acquired. As if sanctity and mysticism were "goods" that one must have in order to be acceptable in the Kingdom of God—just as one must have a new car every two years, a ranch house and a TV set in order to be acceptable in the cities of men. The new car and all that goes with it seem to indicate that one is not a bum or a slacker. That one is faithful to all the accepted standards. So too, spiritual consolations and very obvious virtues are supposed to be the sign that one has worked loyally in the service of God.

Little do we realize the meaning of spiritual poverty, of emptiness, of desolation, of total abandonment in the mystical life. Contemplative experience is not arrived at by the accumulation of grandiose thoughts and visions or by the practice of heroic mortifications. It is not "something you can buy" with any coin, however spiritual it might seem to be. It is a pure Gift of God, and it *has to be* a gift, for that is part of its very essence. It is a gift of which we can never, by any action of ours, make ourselves fully and strictly worthy. Indeed, contemplation itself is not necessarily a sign of worthiness or sanctity at all. It is a sign of the goodness of God, and it enables us to believe more firmly in His goodness, to trust in Him more, above all to be more faithful in our friendship with Him. All these should normally grow up as the fruits of contemplation. But do not be surprised if contemplation springs out of pure emptiness, in poverty, dereliction and spiritual night.

In point of fact, too ardent a desire for contemplation can be an obstacle to contemplation, because it may proceed from delusion and attachment to one's self. The very desire for contemplation may be a dense, opaque, heavy thing that fills our emptiness, enslaves us to the idol of our exterior self, and binds us, like blind Samson, to the mill of vain hopes and illusory desires.

BE careful of every vain hope: it is in reality a temptation to despair. It may seem very real, very substantial. You may come to depend far too much on this apparent solidity of what you think is soon to be yours. You may make your whole spiritual life, your very faith itself, depend on this illusory promise. Then, when it dissolves into air, everything else dissolves along with it. Your whole spiritual life slips away between your fingers and you are left with nothing.

In reality, this could be a good thing, and we should be able to regard it as a good thing, if only we could fall back on the substantiality of pure and obscure faith, which cannot deceive us. But our faith is weak. Indeed, too often the weakest thing about our faith is the illusion that our faith is strong, when the "strength" we feel is only the intensity of emotion or of sentiment, which have nothing to do with real faith.

How many people there are in the world of today who have "lost their faith" along with the vain hopes and illusions of their childhood. What they called "faith" was just one among all the other illusions. They placed all their hope in a certain sense of spiritual peace, of comfort, of interior equilibrium, of self-respect. Then when they began to struggle with the real difficulties and burdens of mature life, when they became aware of their own weakness, they lost their peace, they let go of their precious self-respect, and it became impossible for them to "believe." That is to say it became impossible for them to comfort themselves, to reassure themselves, with the images and concepts that they found reassuring in childhood.

Place no hope in the feeling of assurance, in spiritual comfort. You may well have to get along without this. Place no hope in the inspirational preachers of Christian sunshine, who are able to pick you up and set you back on your feet and make you feel good for three or four days—until you fold up and collapse into despair.

Self-confidence is a precious natural gift, a sign of health. But it is not the same thing as faith. Faith is much deeper, and it must be deep enough to subsist when we are weak, when we are sick, when our self-confidence is gone, when our self-respect is gone. I do not mean that faith *only* functions when we are otherwise in a state of collapse. But true faith must be able to go on even when everything else is taken away from us. Only a humble man is able to accept faith on these terms, so completely without reservation that he is glad of it in its pure state, and welcomes it happily even when nothing else comes with it, and when everything else is taken away.

If we are not humble, we tend to demand that faith must also bring with it good health, peace of mind, good luck, success in business, popularity, world peace, and every other good thing we can imagine. And it is true that God can give us all these good things if He wants to. But they are of no importance compared with faith, which is essential. If we insist on other things as the price of our believing, we tend by that very fact to undermine our own belief. I do not think it would be an act of mercy on God's part simply to let us get away with this!

A HUMBLE man is not disturbed by praise. Since he is no longer concerned with himself, and since he knows where the good that is in him comes from, he does not refuse praise, because it belongs to the God he loves, and in receiving it he keeps nothing for himself but gives it all, with great joy, to his God. *Fecit mihi qui potens est, et sanctum nomen ejus!*

A man who is not humble cannot accept praise gracefully. He knows what he ought to do about it. He knows that the praise belongs to God and not to himself: but he passes it on to God so clumsily that he trips himself up and draws attention to himself by his own awkwardness.

One who has not yet learned humility becomes upset and disturbed by praise. He may even lose his patience when people praise him; he is irritated by the sense of his own unworthiness. And if he does not make a fuss about it, at least the things that have been said about him haunt him and obsess his mind. They torment him wherever he goes.

At the other extreme is the man who has no humility at all and who devours praise, if he gets any, the way a dog gobbles a chunk of meat. But he presents no problem: he is so obvious that he has been a character in every farce since Aristophanes.

The humble man receives praise the way a clean window takes the light of the sun. The truer and more intense the light is, the less you see of the glass.

THERE is danger that men in monasteries will go to such elaborate efforts to be humble, with the humility they have learned from a book, that they will make true humility impossible. How can you be humble if you are always paying attention to yourself? True humility excludes self-consciousness, but false humility intensifies our awareness of ourselves to such a point that we are crippled, and can no longer make any movement or perform any action without putting to work a whole complex mechanism of apologies and formulas of self-accusation.

If you were truly humble you would not bother about yourself at all. Why should you? You would only be concerned with God and with His will and with the objective order of things and values as they are, and not as your selfishness wants them to be. Consequently you would have no more illusions to defend. Your movements would be free. You would not need to be hampered with excuses which are really only framed to defend you against the accusation of pride—as if your humility depended on what other people thought of you!

A humble man can do great things with an uncommon perfection because he is no longer concerned about incidentals, like his own interests and his own reputation, and therefore he no longer needs to waste his efforts in defending them.

For a humble man is not afraid of failure. In fact, he is not afraid of anything, even of himself, since perfect humility implies perfect confidence in the power of God, before whom no other power has any meaning and for whom there is no such thing as an obstacle.

Humility is the surest sign of strength.

26

Freedom under Obedience

VERY few men are sanctified in isolation. Very few become perfect in absolute solitude.

Living with other people and learning to lose ourselves in the understanding of their weakness and deficiencies can help us to become true contemplatives. For there is no better means of getting rid of the rigidity and harshness and coarseness of our ingrained egoism, which is the one insuperable obstacle to the infused light and action of the Spirit of God.

Even the courageous acceptance of interior trials in utter solitude cannot altogether compensate for the work of purification accomplished in us by patience and humility in loving other men and sympathizing with their most unreasonable needs and demands.

There is always a danger that hermits will only dry up and solidify in their own eccentricity. Living out of touch with other people they tend to lose that deep sense of spiritual realities which only pure love can give.

Do you think the way to sanctity is to lock yourself up with your prayers and your books and the meditations that please and interest your mind, to protect yourself, with many walls, against people you consider stupid? Do you think the way to contemplation is found in the refusal of activities and works which are necessary for the good of others but which happen to bore and distract you? Do you imagine that you will discover God by winding yourself up in a cocoon of spiritual and aesthetic pleasures, instead of renouncing all your tastes and desires and ambitions and satisfactions for the love of Christ, who will not even live within you if you cannot find Him in other men?

FAR from being essentially opposed to each other, interior contemplation and external activity are two aspects of the same love of God.

But the activity of a contemplative must be born of his contemplation and must resemble it. Everything he does outside of contemplation ought to reflect the luminous tranquillity of his interior life.

To this end, he will have to look for the same thing in his activity as he finds in his contemplation—contact and union with God.

No matter how little you may have learned of God in prayer, compare your acts with that little: order them by that measure. Try to make all your activity bear fruit in the same emptiness and silence and detachment you have found in contemplation. Ultimately the secret of all this is perfect abandonment to the will of God in things you cannot control, and perfect obedience to Him in everything that depends on your own volition, so that in all things, in your interior life and in your outward works for God, you desire only one thing, which is the fulfilment of His will.

If you do this, your activity will share the disinterested peace that you are able to find at prayer, and in the simplicity of the things you do men will recognize your peacefulness and will give glory to God.

It is above all in this silent and unconscious testimony to the love of God that the contemplative exercises his apostolate. For the saint preaches sermons by the way he walks and the way he stands and the way he sits down and the way he picks things up and holds them in his hand.

The perfect do not have to reflect on the details of their actions.

Less and less conscious of themselves, they finally cease to be aware of themselves doing things, and gradually God begins to do all that they do, in them and for them, at least in the sense that the habit of His love has become second nature to them and informs all that they do with His likeness.

THE extreme difficulties that lie in the way of those who seek interior freedom and purity of love soon teach them that they cannot advance by themselves, and the Spirit of God gives them a desire for the simplest means of overcoming their own selfishness and blindness of judgment. And this is obedience to the judgment and guidance of another.

A spirit that is drawn to God in contemplation will soon learn the value of obedience: the hardships and anguish he has to suffer every day from the burden of his own selfishness, his clumsiness, incompetence and pride will give him a hunger to be led and advised and directed by somebody else.

His own will becomes the source of so much misery and so much darkness that he does not go to some other man merely to seek light, or wisdom, or counsel: he comes to have a passion for obedience itself and for the renunciation of his own will and of his own lights.

Therefore he does not obey his abbot or his director merely because the commands or the advice given to him seem good and profitable and intelligent in his own eyes. He does not obey just because he thinks the abbot makes admirable decisions. On the contrary, sometimes the decisions of his superior seem to be less wise: but with this he is no longer concerned, because he accepts the superior as a mediator between him and God and rests only in the will of God as it comes to him through the men that have been placed over him by the circumstances of his vocation.

F

THE most dangerous man in the world is the contemplative who is guided by nobody. He trusts his own visions. He obeys the attractions of an interior voice but will not listen to other men. He identifies the will of God with anything that makes him feel, within his own heart, a big, warm, sweet interior glow. The sweeter and the warmer the feeling is the more he is convinced of his own infallibility. And if the sheer force of his own self-confidence communicates itself to other people and gives them the impression that he is really a saint, such a man can wreck a whole city or a religious order or even a nation. The world is covered with scars that have been left in its flesh by visionaries like these.

However, very often these people are nothing more than harmless bores. They have wandered into a spiritual blind-alley and there they rest in a snug little nest of private emotions. No one else can really bring himself either to envy or admire them, because even those who know nothing of the spiritual life can somehow sense that these are men who have cheated themselves out of reality and have come to be content with a fake.

They seem to be happy, but there is nothing inspiring or contagious about their happiness. They seem to be at peace, but their peace is hollow and restless. They have much to say, and everything they say is a message with a capital "M," and yet it convinces nobody. Because they have preferred pleasure and emotion to the austere sacrifices imposed by genuine faith, their souls have become stagnant. The flame of true contemplation has gone out.

When you are led by God into the darkness where contemplation is found, you are not able to rest in the false sweetness of your own will. The fake interior satisfaction of self-complacency and absolute confidence in your own judgment will never be able to deceive you entirely: it will make you slightly sick and you will be forced by a vague sense of interior nausea to gash yourself open and let the poison out.

In order to understand the true value of spiritual obedience
we must be very careful to distinguish between self-will and
genuine liberty. This distinction is a matter of great importance,
because we are called to freedom under obedience and not to
the mere sacrifice of all freedom in order to respond to authority
like machines. The highest freedom is found in obedience to
God. The loss of freedom lies in subjection to the tyranny of
automatism, whether in the capriciousness of our own self-
will or in the blind dictates of despotism, convention, routine
or mere collective inertia.

One of the most common of illusions is that by asserting
my own caprices against the dictates of authority, I am mani-
festing my own freedom. I am acting "spontaneously." This is
not true spontaneity, and it does not lead to genuine freedom.
It is licence rather than liberty. Of course, even this imperfect
spontaneity may be in itself preferable to the dead routine of
passive conventionalism, but this should not keep us from
seeing its obvious limitations.

Yet today people have great difficulty in understanding
religious obedience, precisely because it is felt that the sacrifice
of "one's own personality" and of one's "spontaneity" is too
much to ask. In reality, the issues are often terribly confused.
On the one hand, the subject may be flying from responsibility.
On the other, the superior may be governed by caprice and
immaturity, being himself imperfectly able to cope with the
responsibilities of his position.

Only someone who has himself really learned to obey
intelligently is capable of assuming intelligent command.
When he does so, he knows the true value of obedience for
the subject as well as the strict limitation of his own powers.
Once it is frankly admitted that the prudence of the superior

and his real capacity to assume the responsibilities of his position are of great importance, we must also remember that the subject must know how to obey the superior he actually has, whether or not the latter is fully capable. The subject may or may not be aware that his situation is not quite ideal. But this awareness should in no way affect his willingness to obey. Charity demands that he overlook any deficiencies in the one placed over him and common sense dictates a certain hesitation to criticize and analyse the Superior's decisions. After all, no man is a judge in his own cause, and we are very likely to be moved by prejudice and self-will to see deficiencies that are not really there. Hence, while not blinding ourselves deliberately to the truth, we must be convinced that it is very profitable for us to exercise ourselves in obedience even to commands that are not always perfectly rational or prudent. In doing this we are not blinding ourselves or telling ourselves lies about the case. We simply accept the situation as it is, with all its defects, and obey for the love of God. In order to do so we have to make a fully rational and free decision which, in some cases, may be extremely difficult.

No one can become a saint or a contemplative merely by abandoning himself unintelligently to an oversimplified concept of obedience. Both in the subject and in the one commanding him, obedience presupposes a large element of prudence and prudence means responsibility. Obedience is not the abdication of freedom but its *prudent use* under certain well-defined conditions. This does nothing to make obedience easier and it is by no means an escape from subjection to authority. On the contrary, obedience of this kind implies a mature mind able to make difficult decisions and to correctly understand difficult commands, carrying them out fully with a fidelity that can be, at times, genuinely heroic. Such obedience is impossible without deep resources of mature spiritual love.

27

What is Liberty?

THE mere ability to choose between good and evil is the lowest limit of freedom, and the only thing that is free about it is the fact that we can still choose good.

To the extent that you are free to choose evil, you are not free. An evil choice destroys freedom.

We can never choose evil as evil: only as an apparent good. But when we decide to do something that seems to us to be good when it is not really so, we are doing something that we do not really want to do, and therefore we are not really free.

PERFECT spiritual freedom is a total inability to make any evil choice. When everything you desire is truly good and every choice not only aspires to that good but attains it, then you are free because you do everything that you want, every act of your will ends in perfect fulfilment.

Freedom therefore does not consist in an equal balance between good and evil choices but in the perfect love and acceptance of what is really good and the perfect hatred and rejection of what is evil, so that everything you do is good and makes you happy, and you refuse and deny and ignore every possibility that might lead to unhappiness and self-deception and grief. Only the man who has rejected all evil so completely that he is unable to desire it at all is truly free.

GOD, in whom there is absolutely no shadow or possibility of evil or of sin, is infinitely free. In fact, He is Freedom.

Only the will of God is indefectible. Every other freedom can fail and defeat itself by a false choice. All true freedom comes to us as a supernatural gift of God, as a participation in His own essential Freedom by the love He infuses into our souls, uniting them with Him first in perfect consent, then in a transforming union of wills.

The other freedom, the so-called freedom of our nature, which is indifference with respect to good and evil choices, is nothing more than a capacity, a potentiality waiting to be fulfilled by the grace, the will and the supernatural love of God.

ALL good, all perfection, all happiness, are found in the infinitely good and perfect and blessed will of God. Since true freedom means the ability to desire and choose, always, without error, without defection, what is really good, then freedom can only be found in perfect union and submission to the will of God. If our will travels with His, it will reach the same end, rest in the same peace, and be filled with the same infinite happiness that is His.

Therefore, the simplest definition of freedom is this: it means the ability to do the will of God. To be able to resist His will is not to be free. In sin there is no true freedom.

SURROUNDING sin there are certain goods—in sins of the flesh there are, for instance, pleasures of the flesh. But it is not these pleasures that are evil. They are good, and they are willed by God and even when someone takes those pleasures in a way that is not God's will, God still wills that those pleasures should be felt. But though the pleasures in themselves are good, the direction of the will to them under circumstances that are against the will of God, becomes evil. And because that direction of the will is evil it cannot reach the mark which the will intends. Therefore it defeats itself. And therefore there is ultimately no happiness in any act of sin.

You fool! You have really done what you did not want to do! God has left you with the pleasure, because the pleasure also was His will: but you have neglected the happiness He wanted to give you along with the pleasure, or perhaps the greater happiness He intended for you *without* the pleasure and beyond it and above it!

You have eaten the rind and thrown away the orange. You have kept the paper that was nothing but a wrapping and you have thrown away the case and the ring and the diamond.

And now that the pleasure—which has to end—is finished, you have nothing of the happiness that would have enriched you forever. If you had taken (or forsaken) the pleasure in the way God willed for the sake of your happiness, you would still possess the pleasure in your happiness, and it would be with you always and follow you everywhere in God's will. For it is impossible for a sane man to seriously regret an act that was consciously performed in union with God's will.

Liberty, then, is a talent given us by God, an instrument to work with. It is the tool with which we build our own lives, our own happiness. Our true liberty is something we must never sacrifice, for if we sacrifice it we renounce God Himself. Only the false spontaneity of caprice, the pseudo liberty of sin is to be sacrificed. Our true liberty must be defended with life itself for it is the most precious element in our being. It is our liberty that makes us Persons, constituted in the divine image. The supernatural society of the Church has, as one of its chief functions, the preservation of our spiritual liberty as sons of God. How few people realize this!

28

Detachment

I WONDER if there are twenty men alive in the world now who see things as they really are. That would mean there were twenty men who were free, who were not dominated or even influenced by any attachment to any created thing or to their own selves or to any gift of God, even to the highest, the most supernaturally pure of His graces. I don't believe that there are twenty such men alive in the world. But there must be one or two. They are the ones who are holding everything together and keeping the universe from falling apart.

EVERYTHING you love for its own sake, outside of God alone, blinds your intellect and destroys your judgment of moral values. It vitiates your choices so that you cannot clearly distinguish good from evil and you do not truly know God's will.

When you love and desire things for their own sakes, even though you may understand general moral principles, you do not know how to apply them. Even when your application of principles is formally correct, there will probably be a hidden circumstance you have overlooked, which will spoil your most virtuous actions with some imperfection.

As for those who have thrown themselves entirely into the disorder of sin—they often make themselves incapable of understanding the simplest principles; they can no longer see the most obvious and the most natural moral law. They may have the most brilliant gifts and be able to discuss the subtlest of ethical questions—and they do not even have a faint appreciation of what they are talking about because they have no love for these things as values, only an abstract interest in them as concepts.

THERE are aspects of detachment and refinements of interior purity and delicacy of conscience that even the majority of sincerely holy men never succeed in discovering. Even in the strictest monasteries and in places where people have seriously dedicated their lives to the search for perfection, many never come to suspect how much they are governed by unconscious forms of selfishness, how much their virtuous acts are prompted by a narrow and human self-interest. In fact, it is often precisely the rigidity and the unbending formalism of these pious men that keep them from becoming truly detached.

They have given up the pleasures and ambitions of the world, but they have acquired for themselves other pleasures and ambitions which have a higher and more subtle and more spiritual character. Sometimes they never even dream that it is possible to seek perfection with an intensity of self-conscious zeal that is itself imperfect. They too are attached to the good things of their little enclosed world.

Sometimes, for instance, a monk can develop an attachment to prayer or fasting, or to a pious practice or devotion, or to a certain external penance, or to a book or to a system of spirituality or to a method of meditation or even to contemplation itself, to the highest graces of prayer, to virtues, to things that are in themselves marks of heroism and high sanctity. And men who seemed to be saints have let themselves be blinded by their inordinate love for such things. They have remained almost as much in darkness and error as brothers in the monastery who seemed far less perfect than they.

SOMETIMES contemplatives think that the whole end and essence of their life is to be found in recollection and interior peace and the sense of the presence of God. They become attached to these things. But recollection is just as much a creature as an automobile. The sense of interior peace is no less created than a bottle of wine. The experimental "awareness" of the presence of God is just as truly a created thing as a glass of beer. The only difference is that recollection and interior peace and the sense of the presence of God are spiritual pleasures and the others are material. Attachment to spiritual things is therefore just as much an attachment as inordinate love of anything else. The imperfection may be more hidden and more subtle: but from a certain point of view that only makes it all the more harmful because it is not so easy to recognize.

And so, many contemplatives never become great saints, never enter into close friendship with God, never find a deep participation in His immense joys, because they cling to the miserable little consolations that are given to beginners in the contemplative way.

How many there are who are in a worse state still: they never even get as far as contemplation because they are attached to activities and enterprises that seem to be important. Blinded by their desire for ceaseless motion, for a constant sense of achievement, famished with a crude hunger for results, for visible and tangible success, they work themselves into a state in which they cannot believe that they are pleasing God unless they are busy with a dozen jobs at the same time. Sometimes they fill the air with lamentations and complain that they no longer have any time for prayer, but they have become such experts in deceiving themselves that they do not realize how insincere their lamentations are. They not only allow themselves to be involved in more and more work, they actually go looking for new jobs. And the busier they become the more mistakes they make. Accidents and errors pile up all around them. They will not be warned. They get further and further away from reality—and then perhaps God allows their mistakes to catch up with them. Then they wake up and discover that their carelessness has involved them in some gross and obvious sin against justice, for instance, or against the obligations of their state. So, having no interior strength left, they fall apart.

How many there must be who have smothered the first sparks of contemplation by piling wood on the fire before it was well lit. The stimulation of interior prayer so excites them that they launch out into ambitious projects for teaching and converting the whole world, when all that God asks of them is to be quiet and keep themselves at peace, attentive to the secret work He is beginning in their souls.

And yet if you try to explain to them that there might be a considerable imperfection in their zeal for activities that God does not desire of them, they will treat you as a heretic. They know you must be wrong because they feel such an intense appetite for the results which they imagine they are going to accomplish.

THE secret of interior peace is detachment. Recollection is impossible for the man who is dominated by all the confused and changing desires of his own will. And even if those desires reach out for the good things of the interior life, for recollection, for peace, for the pleasures of prayer, if they are no more than the natural and selfish desires they will make recollection difficult and even impossible.

You will never be able to have perfect interior peace and recollection unless you are detached even from the desire of peace and recollection. You will never be able to pray perfectly until you are detached from the pleasures of prayer.

If you give up all these desires and seek one thing only, God's will, He will give you recollection and peace in the middle of labour and conflict and trial.

THERE is a kind of crude materialism in religious life which makes sincerely holy men believe that abnegation means simply giving up things that please the five exterior senses.

But that is scarcely the beginning of abnegation.

Of course we have to be detached from gross and sensual things before the interior life can even begin. But once it has begun it will make little progress unless we become more and more detached even from rational and intellectual and spiritual goods.

A man who hopes to become a contemplative by detaching himself only from the things that are forbidden by reason will not even begin to know the meaning of contemplation. For the way to God lies through deep darkness in which all knowledge and all created wisdom and all pleasure and prudence and all human hope and human joy are defeated and annulled by the overwhelming purity of the light and the presence of God.

It is not enough to possess and enjoy material and spiritual things within the limits of rational moderation: we must be able to rise above all joy and pass beyond all possession if we will come to the pure possession and enjoyment of God.

This distinction is very important and yet it is often forgotten even by spiritual writers. It is quite true, of course, that God's creatures are all good and that our moderate, temperate use of them brings us to closer union with Him. It is also true that those who are most closely united to Him and detached from their exterior self are able to taste the purest joy in the beauty of created things, which is no longer an obstacle to the light of God.

But in between the temperate use of created things, the virtuous life of reasonable moderation, and the totally spirit-ualized purity of the saint, which is like a recovery of Adam's innocence in Paradise, in the world's childhood, there lies an abyss which can only be crossed by a blind leap of ascetic detachment.

Beyond rational temperance there comes a sacrificial death which is on a higher level than mere virtue or practised discipline. Here the Cross of Christ enters into the life of the contemplative. Without the mystical death that completely separates him from created things, there is no perfect freedom and no advance into the promised land of mystical union.

But this "death" of sense and of spirit, which brings the final liberation from attachment, is not the fruit of man's own ascetic effort alone. The Dark Night, the crisis of suffering that rends our roots out of this world, is a pure gift of God. Yet it is also a gift which we must in some degree prepare ourselves to receive by heroic acts of self-denial. For unless it is clear that we mean seriously to undertake a *total renunciation of all attachments*, the Holy Spirit will not lead us into the true darkness, the heart of mystical desolation, in which God Himself mysteriously liberates us from confusion, from the multiplicity of needs and desires, in order to give us unity in and with Himself.

In a word, we must face with great resoluteness the task of going beyond ordinary temperance and strive for complete emptiness if we seek to pass beyond the limitations of human virtuousness and enter into the perfect freedom of the sons of God, for whom all things are light and joy because all are seen and tasted in and for God. The mystic lives in emptiness, in freedom, as if he had no longer a limited and exclusive "self" that distinguished him from God and other men. He has, therefore, died with Christ and entered into the "risen life" promised to the true sons of God. Even the joys of the lower levels of contemplation must themselves be renounced by anyone who seeks to pass over into the Promised Land.

AND so the true contemplative life does not consist in the enjoyment of interior and spiritual pleasures. Contemplation is something more than a refined and holy aestheticism of the intellect and of the will, in love and faith. To rest in the beauty of God as a pure concept, without the accidents of image or sensible species or any other representation, is a pleasure which still belongs to the human order. It is perhaps the highest pleasure to which nature has access and many people do not arrive at it by their natural powers alone—they need grace before they can experience this satisfaction which is of itself within the reach of nature. And nevertheless, since it is natural and can be desired by nature and acquired by natural disciplines, it must not be confused with supernatural contemplation.

True contemplation is the work of a love that transcends all satisfaction and all experience to rest in the night of pure and naked faith. This faith brings us so close to God that it may be said to touch and grasp Him as He is, though in darkness. And the effect of such a contact is often a deep peace that overflows into the lower faculties of the soul and thus constitutes an "experience." Yet that experience or feeling of peace always remains an accident of contemplation, so that the absence of this "sense" does not mean that our contact with God has ceased.

To become attached to the "experience" of peace is to threaten the true and essential and vital union of our soul with God above sense and experience in the darkness of a pure and perfect love.

And so, although this sense of peace may be a sign that we are united to God, it is still only a sign—an accident. The substance of the union may be had without any such sense, and sometimes when we have no feeling of peace or of God's presence He is more truly present to us than He has ever been before.

If we attach too much importance to these accidentals we will run the risk of losing what is essential, which is the perfect acceptance of God's will, whatever our feelings may happen to be.

But if I think the most important thing in life is a feeling of interior peace, I will be all the more disturbed when I notice that I do not have it. And since I cannot directly produce that feeling in myself whenever I want to, the disturbance will increase with the failure of my efforts. Finally I will lose my patience by refusing to accept this situation which I cannot control and so I will let go of the one important reality, union with the will of God, without which true peace is completely impossible.

When we consider the fidelity, the resoluteness, the determination to renounce all things for the love of God, without which we cannot pass over to the higher levels of purity and contemplation, we remain aghast at our own weakness, our own poverty, our evasions, our infidelity, our hesitancy. Our very weakness clouds our vision. We are left helpless, knowing very well that we are asked to give up everything, yet not knowing how or where to begin. In such a condition there is no use in forcing the issue. Great patience and humility are needed, and humble prayer for light, courage and strength.

If we resolutely face our cowardice and confess it to God, no doubt He will one day take pity on us, and show us the way to freedom in detachment.

29

Mental Prayer

SINCE contemplation is the union of our mind and will with God in an act of pure love that brings us into obscure contact with Him as He really is, the way to contemplation is to develop and perfect our mind and will and our whole soul. Infused contemplation begins when the direct intervention of God raises this whole process of development above the level of our nature: and then He perfects our faculties by seeming to defeat all their activity in the suffering and darkness of His infused light and love.

But before this begins, we ordinarily have to labour to prepare ourselves in our own way and with the help of His grace, by deepening our knowledge and love of God in meditation and active forms of prayer, as well as by setting our wills free from attachment to created things.

About all these things many books have been written. There are all kinds of techniques and methods of meditation and mental prayer, and it would be hard to begin to talk about them all. That is why I shall talk about none of them except to say that they are all good for those who can use them, and everyone who can get profit out of systematic meditation should not fail to do so, as long as he is not afraid to lay the method aside and do a little thinking for himself once in a while.

The trouble with all these methods is not that they are too systematic and too formal: they need to be both these things, and it is good that they are. There is nothing wrong with methods. The trouble lies in the way people use them—or fail to use them.

The purpose of a book of meditations is to teach you how to think and not to do your thinking for you. Consequently if you pick up such a book and simply read it through, you are wasting your time. As soon as any thought stimulates your mind or your heart you can put the book down because your meditation has begun. To think that you are somehow obliged to follow the author of the book to his own particular conclusion would be a great mistake. It may happen that his conclusion does not apply to you. God may want you to end up somewhere else. He may have planned to give you quite a different grace than the one the author suggests you might be needing.

And then there are people who only think of meditating when the book is explicitly called "Meditations." If you called it something else they would assume they were just supposed to read it without attempting to think.

The best thing beginners in the spiritual life can do, after they have really acquired the discipline of mind that enables them to concentrate on a spiritual subject and get below the surface of its meaning and incorporate it into their own lives, is to acquire the agility and freedom of mind that will help them to find light and warmth and ideas and love for God everywhere they go and in all that they do. People who only know how to think about God during fixed periods of the day will never get very far in the spiritual life. In fact, they will not even think of Him in the moments they have religiously marked off for "mental prayer."

LEARN how to meditate on paper. Drawing and writing are forms of meditation. Learn how to contemplate works of art. Learn how to pray in the streets or in the country. Know how to meditate not only when you have a book in your hand but when you are waiting for a bus or riding in a train. Above all, enter into the Church's liturgy and make the liturgical cycle

part of your life—let its rhythm work its way into your body
and soul.

THE reason why meditation and mental prayer do not serve
their true purpose in the lives of so many who practise them is
that their true purpose is not really understood.

Some people seem to think that the only reason for meditating on God is to get some interesting ideas about Him. It is
true that one of the elementary purposes of meditation is to
strengthen all our religious convictions and give them a deeper
foundation of faith and understanding: but that is only the
beginning. That is only the threshold of meditation.

Others suppose that the function of meditation is to show us
the necessity for practising virtues and to produce in us the
courage and determination to go ahead and do something
about it. That is true. This is another elementary fruit of
meditation. But it is only another step on the way.

A less serious error—for now we come closer to the truth—
is that meditation is supposed to produce in us greater love
for God. Whether or not this concept is satisfactory depends
on what you mean by loving God. If you think meditation has
done its work when it has made you *say* you love God or *feel*
that you love God, then you are still wrong.

MEDITATION is a twofold discipline that has a twofold function.

First it is supposed to give you sufficient control over your
mind and memory and will to enable you to recollect yourself
and withdraw from exterior things and the business activities
and thoughts and concerns of temporal existence, and second
—this is the real end of meditation—it teaches you how to
become aware of the presence of God; and most of all it aims
at bringing you to a state of almost constant loving attention
to God, and dependence on Him.

The real purpose of meditation is this: to teach a man how to work himself free of created things and temporal concerns, in which he finds only confusion and sorrow, and enter into a conscious and loving contact with God in which he is disposed to receive from God the help he knows he needs so badly, and to pay to God the praise and honour and thanksgiving and love which it has now become his joy to give.

The success of your meditation will not be measured by the brilliant ideas you get or the great resolutions you make or the feelings and emotions that are produced in your exterior senses. You have only really meditated well when you have come, to some extent, to realize God. Yet even that is not quite the thing.

After all, anyone who has tried it is aware that the closer you get to God, the less question there can be of realizing Him or anything about Him.

And so, suppose your meditation takes you to the point where you are baffled and repelled by the cloud that surrounds God, "who maketh darkness His covert." Far from realizing Him, you begin to realize nothing more than your own helplessness to know Him, and you begin to think that meditation is something altogether hopeless and impossible. And yet the more helpless you are, the more you seem to desire to see Him and to know Him. The tension between your desires and your failure generate in you a painful longing for God which nothing seems able to satisfy.

Do you think your meditation has failed? On the contrary: this bafflement, this darkness, this anguish of helpless desire is a fulfilment of meditation. For if meditation aims above all at establishing in your soul a vital contact of love with the living God, then as long as it only produces images and ideas and affections that you can understand, feel and appreciate, it is not yet doing its full quota of work. But when it gets beyond the level of your understanding and your imagination, it is really bringing you close to God, for it introduces you into the darkness where you can no longer think of Him, and are consequently forced to reach out for Him by blind faith and hope and love.

It is then that you should strengthen yourself against the thought of giving up mental prayer; you should return to it at your appointed time each day, in spite of the difficulty and dryness and pain you feel. Eventually your own suffering and the secret work of grace will teach you what to do.

You may perhaps be led into a completely simple form of affective prayer in which your will, with few words or none, reaches out into the darkness where God is hidden, with a kind of mute, half-hopeless and yet supernaturally confident desire of knowing and loving Him.

Or else, perhaps, knowing by faith that He is present to you and realizing the utter hopelessness of trying to think intelligibly about this immense reality and all that it can mean, you relax in a simple contemplative gaze that keeps your attention peacefully aware of Him hidden somewhere in this deep cloud into which you also feel yourself drawn to enter.

From then on you should keep your prayer as simple as possible.

When it becomes possible to meditate again, meditate. If you get an idea, develop it, but without excitement. Feed your mind with reading and the liturgy, and if the darkness of your simple prayer becomes too much of a tension—or degenerates into torpor or sleep—relieve it with a few vocal prayers or simple affections, but do not strain yourself trying to get ideas or feel fervour. Do not upset yourself with useless efforts to realize the elaborate prospects suggested by a conventional book of meditations.

30

Distractions

PRAYER and love are really learned in the hour when prayer becomes impossible and your heart turns to stone.

IF you have never had any distractions you don't know how to pray. For the secret of prayer is a hunger for God and for the vision of God, a hunger that lies far deeper than the level of language or affection. And a man whose memory and imagination are persecuting him with a crowd of useless or even evil thoughts and images may sometimes be forced to pray far better, in the depths of his murdered heart, than one whose mind is swimming with clear concepts and brilliant purposes and easy acts of love.

That is why it is useless to get upset when you cannot shake off distractions. In the first place, you must realize that they are often unavoidable in the life of prayer. The necessity of kneeling and suffering submersion under a tidal wave of wild and inane images is one of the standard trials of the contemplative life. If you think you are obliged to stave these things off by using a book and clutching at its sentences the way a drowning man clutches at straws, you have the privilege of doing so, but if you allow your prayer to degenerate into a period of simple spiritual reading you are losing a great deal of fruit. You would profit much more by patiently resisting distractions and learning something of your own helplessness and incapacity. And if your book merely becomes an anaesthetic, far from helping your meditation it has probably ruined it.

ONE reason why you have distractions is this. The mind and memory and imagination only work, in meditation, in order to bring your will into the presence of its object, which is God. Now when you have practised meditation for a few years, it is the most spontaneous thing in the world for the will to settle down to its occupation of obscurely and mutely loving God as soon as you compose yourself for prayer. Consequently the mind and memory and imagination have no real job to do. The will is busy and they are unemployed. So, after a while, the doors of your subconscious mind fall ajar and all sorts of curious figures begin to come waltzing about on the scene. If you are wise you will not pay any attention to these things: remain in simple attention to God and keep your will peacefully directed to Him in simple desire, while the intermittent shadows of this annoying movie go about in the remote background. If you are aware of them at all it is only to realize that you refuse them.

The kind of distractions that holy people most fear are generally the most harmless of all. But sometimes pious men and women torture themselves at meditation because they imagine they are "consenting" to the phantasms of a lewd and somewhat idiotic burlesque that is being fabricated in their imagination without their being able to do a thing to stop it. The chief reason why they suffer is that their hopeless efforts to put a stop to this parade of images generate a nervous tension which only makes everything a hundred times worse.

If they ever had a sense of humour, they have now become so nervous that it has abandoned them altogether. Yet humour is one of the things that would probably be most helpful at such a time.

There is no real danger in these things. The distractions that do harm are the ones that draw our will away from its profound and peaceful occupation with God and involve it in elaborations of projects that have been concerning us during our day's work. We are confronted by issues that really attract and occupy our wills and there is considerable danger that our meditation will break down into a session of mental letter-writing or sermons or speeches or books or, worse still, plans to raise money or to take care of our health.

It will be hard for anyone who has a heavy job on his shoulders to get rid of these things. They will always remind him of what he is, and they should warn him not to get too involved in active work, because it is no use trying to clear your mind of all material things at the moment of meditation, if you do nothing to cut down the pressure of work outside that time.

But in all these things, it is the will to pray that is the essence of prayer, and the desire to find God, to see Him and to love Him is the one thing that matters. If you have desired to know Him and love Him, you have already done what was expected of you, and it is much better to desire God without being able to think clearly of Him, than to have marvellous thoughts about Him without desiring to enter into union with His will.

No matter how distracted you may be, pray by peaceful, even perhaps inarticulate, efforts to centre your heart upon God, who is present to you in spite of all that may be going through your mind. His presence does not depend on your thoughts of Him. He is unfailingly there; if He were not, you could not even exist. The memory of His unfailing presence is the surest anchor for our minds and hearts in the storm of distraction and temptation by which we must be purified.

31

The Gift of Understanding

CONTEMPLATION, by which we know and love God as He is in Himself, apprehending Him in a deep and vital experience which is beyond the reach of any natural understanding, is the reason for our creation by God. And although it is absolutely above our nature, St. Thomas teaches that it is our proper element because it is the fulfilment of deep capacities in us that God has willed should never be fulfilled in any other way. All those who reach the end for which they were created will therefore be contemplatives in heaven: but many are also destined to enter this supernatural element and breathe this new atmosphere while they are still on earth.

Since contemplation has been planned for us by God as our true and proper element, the first taste of it strikes us at once as utterly new and yet strangely familiar.

Although you had an entirely different notion of what it would be like (since no book can give an adequate idea of contemplation except to those who have experienced it), it turns out to be just what you seem to have known all along that it ought to be.

The utter simplicity and obviousness of the infused light which contemplation pours into our soul suddenly awakens us to a new level of awareness. We enter a region which we had never even suspected, and yet it is this new world which seems familiar and obvious. The old world of our senses is now the one that seems to us strange, remote and unbelievable—

until the intense light of contemplation leaves us and we fall
back to our own level.

COMPARED with the pure and peaceful comprehension of love
in which the contemplative is permitted to see the truth not so
much by seeing it as by being absorbed into it, ordinary ways of
seeing and knowing are full of blindness and labour and
uncertainty.

The sharpest of natural experiences is like sleep, compared
with the awakening which is contemplation. The keenest and
surest natural certitude is a dream compared to this serene
comprehension.

Our souls rise up from our earth like Jacob waking from his
dream and exclaiming: "Truly God is in this place and I
knew it not"! God Himself becomes the only reality, in whom
all other reality takes its proper place—and falls into insignificance.

Although this light is absolutely above our nature, it now
seems to us "normal" and "natural" to see, as we now see,
without seeing, to possess clarity in darkness, to have pure
certitude without any shred of discursive evidence, to be filled
with an experience that transcends experience and to enter with
serene confidence into depths that leave us utterly inarticulate.

"O the depth of the riches of the wisdom and knowledge of
God!"

A door opens in the centre of our being and we seem to fall
through it into immense depths which, although they are
infinite, are all accessible to us; all eternity seems to have
become ours in this one placid and breathless contact.

God touches us with a touch that is emptiness and empties us.
He moves us with a simplicity that simplifies us. All variety,
all complexity, all paradox, all multiplicity cease. Our mind
swims in the air of an understanding, a reality that is dark and

serene and includes in itself everything. Nothing more is desired. Nothing more is wanting. Our only sorrow, if sorrow be possible at all, is the awareness that we ourselves still live outside of God.

For already a supernatural instinct teaches us that the function of this abyss of freedom that has opened out within our own midst is to draw us utterly out of our own selfhood and into its own immensity of liberty and joy.

You seem to be the same person and you are the same person that you have always been: in fact you are more yourself than you have ever been before. You have only just begun to exist. You feel as if you were at last fully born. All that went before was a mistake, a fumbling preparation for birth. Now you have come into your element. And yet now you have become nothing. You have sunk to the centre of your own poverty, and there you have felt the doors fly open into infinite freedom, into a wealth which is perfect because none of it is yours and yet it all belongs to you.

And now you are free to go in and out of infinity.

It is useless to think of fathoming the depths of wide-open darkness that have yawned inside you, full of liberty and exultation.

They are not a place, not an extent, they are a huge, smooth activity. These depths, they are Love. And in the midst of you they form a wide, impregnable country.

There is nothing that can penetrate into the heart of that peace. Nothing from the outside can get in. There is even a whole sphere of your own activity that is excluded from that beautiful airy night. The five senses, the imagination, the discoursing mind, the hunger of desire do not belong in that starless sky.

And you, while you are free to come and go, yet as soon as you attempt to make words or thoughts about it you are excluded—you go back into your exterior in order to talk.

Yet you find that you can rest in this darkness and this unfathomable peace without trouble and without anxiety, even when the imagination and the mind remain in some way active outside the doors of it.

They may stand and chatter in the porch, as long as they are idle, waiting for the will their queen to return, upon whose orders they depend.

But it is better for them to be silent. However, you now know that this does not depend on you. It is a gift that comes to you from the bosom of that serene darkness and depends entirely on the decision of Love.

Within the simplicity of this armed and walled and undivided interior peace is an infinite unction which, as soon as it is grasped, loses it savour. You must not try to reach out and possess it altogether. You must not touch it, or try to seize it. You must not try to make it sweeter or try to keep it from wasting away. . . .

The situation of the soul in contemplation is something like the situation of Adam and Eve in Paradise. Everything is yours, but on one infinitely important condition: that it is all *given*.

There is nothing you can claim, nothing that you can demand, nothing that you can *take*. And as soon as you try to take something as if it were your own—you lose your Eden. The angel with the flaming sword stands armed against all selfhood that is small and particular, against the "I" that can say "I want . . ." "I need . . ." "I demand. . . ." No individual enters Paradise, only the integrity of the *Person*.

Only the greatest humility can give us the instinctive delicacy and caution that will prevent us from reaching out for pleasures and satisfactions that we can understand and savour in this darkness. The moment we demand anything for ourselves or even trust in any action of our own to procure a deeper intensification of this pure and serene rest in God, we defile and dissipate the perfect gift that He desires to communicate to us in the silence and repose of our own powers.

If there is one thing we must do it is this: we must realize to the very depths of our being that this is a pure gift of God which no desire, no effort and no heroism of ours can do anything to deserve or obtain. There is nothing we can do directly either to procure it or to preserve it or to increase it. Our own activity is for the most part an obstacle to the infusion of this peaceful and pacifying light, with the exception that God may demand certain acts and works of us by charity or obedience, and maintain us in deep experimental union with Him through them all, by His own good pleasure, not by any fidelity of ours.

At best we can dispose ourselves for the reception of this great gift by resting in the heart of our own poverty, keeping our soul as far as possible empty of desires for all the things that please and preoccupy our nature, no matter how pure or sublime they may be in themselves.

And when God reveals Himself to us in contemplation we must accept Him as He comes to us, in His own obscurity, in His own silence, not interrupting Him with arguments or words, conceptions or activities that belong to the level of our own tedious and laboured existence.

We must respond to God's gifts gladly and freely with thanksgiving, happiness and joy: but in contemplation we thank Him less by words than by the serene happiness of silent acceptance. "Be empty and see that I am God." It is our emptiness in the presence of the abyss of His reality, our silence in the presence of His infinitely rich silence, our joy in the bosom of the serene darkness in which His light holds us absorbed, it is all this that praises Him. It is this that causes love of God and wonder and adoration to swim up into us like tidal waves out of the depths

of that peace, and break upon the shores of our consciousness
in a vast, hushed surf of inarticulate praise, praise and glory!

THIS clear darkness of God is the purity of heart Christ spoke
of in the sixth Beatitude. *Beati mundo corde, quoniam ipsi Deum
videbunt.* And this purity of heart brings at least a momentary
deliverance from images and concepts, from the forms and
shadows of all the things men desire with their human appetites.
It brings deliverance even from the feeble and delusive analogies
we ordinarily use to arrive at God—not that it denies them,
for they are true as far as they go, but it makes them temporarily
useless by fulfilling them all in the sure grasp of a deep and
penetrating experience.

IN the vivid darkness of God within us there sometimes come
deep movements of love that deliver us entirely, for a moment,
from our old burden of selfishness, and number us among those
little children of whom is the Kingdom of Heaven.

And when God allows us to fall back into our own confusion
of desires and judgments and temptations, we carry a scar over
the place where that joy exulted for a moment in our hearts.

The scar burns us. The sore wound aches within us, and we
remember that we have fallen back into what we are not, and
are not yet allowed to remain where God would have us
belong. We long for the place He has destined for us and weep
with desire for the time when this pure poverty will catch us
and hold us in its liberty and never let us go, when we will
never fall back from the Paradise of the simple and the little
children into the forum of prudence where the wise of this
world go up and down in sorrow and set their traps for a
happiness that cannot exist.

This is the gift of understanding: we pass out of ourselves
into the joy of emptiness, of nothingness, in which there are no

longer any particular objects of knowledge but only God's truth without limit, without defect, without stain. This clean light, which tastes of Paradise, is beyond all pride, beyond comment, beyond proprietorship, beyond solitude. It is in all, and for all. It is the true light that shines in everyone, in "every man coming into this world." It is the light of Christ, "who stands in the midst of us and we know Him not."

32

The Night of the Senses

THE life of infused contemplation does not always begin with a definite experience of God in a strong inpouring of light. Moments of freedom and escape from the blindness and helplessness of the ordinary, laborious ways of the spirit will always be relatively rare. And it is not too hard to recognize these sudden, intense flashes of understanding, these vivid "rays of darkness" striking deep into the soul and changing the course of a man's whole life. They bring with them their own conviction. They strike blindness from our eyes like scales. They plant in us too deep and too calm and too new a certainty to be misunderstood or quickly forgotten.

But if a man had to wait for such vivid experiences before he became a contemplative he might have to wait a long time—perhaps a whole lifetime. And perhaps his expectation would be vain.

It is more ordinary for the spirit to learn contemplation from God not in a sudden flash but imperceptibly, by very gradual steps. As a matter of fact, without the groundwork of long and patient trial and slow progress in the darkness of pure faith, contemplation will never really be learned at all. For a few isolated, though intense, flashes of the spirit of understanding and wisdom will not make a man a contemplative in the full sense of the word; contemplative prayer is only truly what it is called when it becomes more or less habitual.

At the same time we must remember the curious fact that there are men of prayer who unconsciously come to the threshold of contemplation and remain there without ever realizing where they are. In the first place they do not know how to value or to appreciate this obscure knowledge of God because they imagine that progress in the interior life is progress in clarity, distinct knowledge, and sensible fervour. So it can happen that while they are ready to be "born" as contemplatives they may be imagining that the interior life has, in their case, more or less ended. They feel frustrated and confused. They are, so they believe, at a dead end. Yet perhaps if they can only be patient and humbly remain there, forgetting themselves and trusting in God, they may gradually and quietly come to realize that this is not a dead end at all. They will see that in this apparently dark and frustrated condition they are readjusting themselves, they are being peacefully and gently purified of false hopes and illusory conceptions, and they are being made ready for the journey in the desert which, after many privations, leads at last to the Promised Land.

LET us not forget that the ordinary way to contemplation lies through a desert without trees and without beauty and without water. The spirit enters a wilderness and travels blindly in directions that seem to lead away from vision, away from God, away from all fulfilment and joy. It may become almost impossible to believe that this road goes anywhere at all except to a desolation full of dry bones—the ruin of all our hopes and good intentions.

The prospect of this wilderness is something that so appals most men that they refuse to enter upon its burning sands and travel among its rocks. They cannot believe that contemplation and sanctity are to be found in a desolation where there is no food and no shelter and no refreshment for their imagination and intellect and for the desires of their nature.

Convinced that perfection is to be measured by brilliant intuitions of God and fervent resolutions of a will on fire with love, persuaded that sanctity is a matter of sensible fervour and tangible results, they will have nothing to do with a contemplation that does not delight their reason and invest their minds and wills with consolations and sensible joy. They want to know where they are going and see what they are doing, and as soon as they enter into regions where their own activity becomes paralysed and bears no visible fruit, they turn around and go back to the lush fields where they can be sure that they are doing something and getting somewhere. And if they cannot achieve the results they desire with such intense anxiety, at least they convince themselves that they have made great progress if they have said many prayers, performed many mortifications, preached many sermons, read (and perhaps also written) many books and articles, paged through many books of meditations, acquired hundreds of new and different devotions and girdled the earth with pilgrimages. Not that all of these things are not good in themselves: but there are times in the life of a man when they can become an escape, an anodyne, a refuge from the responsibility of suffering in darkness and obscurity and helplessness, and allowing God to strip us of our false selves and make us into the new men that we are really meant to be.

WHEN God begins to infuse His light of knowledge and understanding into the spirit of a man drawn to contemplation, the experience is often not so much one of fulfilment as of defeat.

The mind finds itself entering uneasily into the shadows of a strange and silent night. The night is peaceful enough. But it is very frustrating. Thought becomes cramped and difficult. There is a peculiarly heavy sense of weariness and distaste for mental and spiritual activity. Yet at the same time the soul is haunted with a fear that this new impotence is a sin, or a sign of imperfection. It tries to force acts of thought and will. Sometimes it makes a mad effort to squeeze some feeling of fervour out of

G

itself, which is, incidentally, the worst thing it could possibly do. All the pretty images and concepts of God that it once cherished have vanished or have turned into unpleasant and frightening distortions. God is nowhere to be found. The words of prayers return in a hollow echo from the walls of this dead cave.

If a man in this night lets his spirit get carried away with fear or impatience and anxiety, he will come to a standstill. He will twist and turn and torture himself with attempts to see some light and feel some warmth and recapture the old consolations that are beyond recovery. And finally he will run away from darkness, and do the best he can to dope himself with the first light that comes along.

But there are others who, no matter how much they suffer perplexity and uneasiness in the wilderness where God begins to lead them, still feel drawn farther and farther on into the wasteland. They cannot think, they cannot meditate; their imagination tortures them with everything they do not want to see; their life of prayer is without light and without pleasure and without any feeling of devotion.

On the other hand they sense, by a kind of instinct, that peace lies in the heart of this darkness. Something prompts them to keep still, to trust in God, to be quiet and listen for His voice; to be patient and not to get excited. Soon they discover that all useless attempts to meditate only upset and disturb them; but at the same time, when they stay quiet in the muteness of naked truth, resting in a simple and open-eyed awareness, attentive to the darkness which baffles them, a subtle and indefinable peace begins to seep into their souls and occupies them with a deep and inexplicable satisfaction. This satisfaction is tenuous and dark. It cannot be grasped or identified. It slips out of focus and gets away. Yet it is there.

What is it? It is hard to say: but one feels that it is somehow summed up in "the will of God" or simply, "God."

33

Journey through the Wilderness

THE man who does not permit his spirit to be beaten down and upset by dryness and helplessness, but who lets God lead him peacefully through the wilderness, and desires no other support or guidance than that of pure faith and trust in God alone, will be brought to the Promised Land. He will taste the peace and joy of union with God. He will, without "seeing," have an habitual, comforting, obscure and mysterious awareness of his God, present and acting in all the events of life.

The man who is not afraid to abandon all his spiritual progress into the hands of God, to put prayer, virtue, merit, grace, and all gifts in the keeping of Him from whom they all must come, will quickly be led to peace in union with Him. His peace will be all the sweeter because it will be free of every care.

JUST as the light of faith is darkness to the mind, so the supreme supernatural activity of the mind and will in contemplation and infused love at first seems to us like inaction. That is why our natural faculties are anxious and restless. That is why they refuse to keep still. They want to be the sole principles of their own acts. The thought that they cannot act according to their own spontaneous impulsion brings them a suffering and humiliation which they find it hard to stand.

But contemplation lifts us beyond the sphere of our natural powers.

When you are travelling in a plane close to the ground you

realize that you are going somewhere: but in the stratosphere, although you may be going seven times as fast, you lose all sense of speed.

As soon as there is any reasonable indication that God is drawing the spirit into this way of contemplation, we ought to remain at peace in a prayer that is utterly simplified, stripped of acts and reflections and clean of images, waiting in emptiness and vigilant expectancy for the will of God to be done in us. This waiting should be without anxiety and without deliberate hunger for any experience that comes within the range of our knowledge or memory, because any experience that we can grasp or understand will be inadequate and unworthy of the state to which God wishes to bring our souls.

The most important practical question that people will ask at this point is: What are the signs that it is safe to abandon formal meditation and rest in this more or less passive expectancy?

In the first place, if meditation and affective prayer are easy, spontaneous and fruitful they should not be given up. But when they have become practically impossible, or if they simply deaden and exhaust the mind and will, and fill them with disgust, or if they involve them in many distractions, it would be harmful to force your mind to have precise thoughts and your will to go through a routine of specified acts. When the imagination (though it may remain quite active) gives you no more pleasure and no more fruit, but only tires and upsets you even when it rests on the most attractive of natural or even spiritual things, it is a sign that perhaps you should give up active meditation. If, at the same time, you find positive peace and derive fruit from resting in a simple and faithful expectation of help from God, it would be better to do that than to persecute your mind and will in a vain effort to beat a few thoughts and affections out of them. For if you reflect on your state, you will easily see that your mind is absorbed in one vast, obscure thought of God and your will is occupied, if not haunted, with a blind, groping, half-defined desire of God. These two combine to produce in you the anxiety and darkness and helplessness which make lucid and particular acts at once so hard and so futile. And if you allow yourself to remain in silence and emptiness you may find that this thirst, this hunger that seeks God in blindness and darkness, will grow on you and at the same time, although you do not yet seem to find anything tangible, peace will establish itself in your soul.

On the other hand, if giving up meditation simply means that your mind goes dead and your will gets petrified, and you lean against the wall and spend your half-hour of meditation wondering what you are going to get for supper, you had better keep yourself occupied with something definite. After all, there is always a possibility that laziness will dress itself up as "prayer of quiet" or "prayer of simplicity" and degenerate into torpor and sleep. The mere absence of activity does not *ipso facto* turn you into a contemplative.

This is where a book may sometimes help you. It is quite normal to use the Bible, or a spiritual book of some kind, to "get started" even in the kind of prayer where you do not do much actual "thinking." When you find some paragraph or sentence that interests you, stop reading and turn it over in your mind and absorb it and contemplate it and rest in the general, serene, effortless consideration of the thought, not in its details but as a whole, as something held and savoured in its entirety: and so pass from this to rest in the quiet expectancy of God. If you find yourself getting distracted, go back to the book, to the same sentence or to another. You can start your mental prayer in this way not only by using a book but also by looking at a picture or a crucifix or best of all in the presence of the Blessed Sacrament, but also out in the woods and under the trees. The sweep and serenity of a landscape, fields and hills, are enough to keep a contemplative riding the quiet interior tide of his peace and his desire for hours at a time.

THE absence of activity in contemplative prayer is only apparent. Below the surface, the mind and will are drawn into the orbit of an activity that is deep and intense and supernatural, and which overflows into our whole being and brings forth incalculable fruits.

There is no such thing as a kind of prayer in which you do absolutely nothing. If you are doing nothing you are not praying. On the other hand, if God is the source of your interior activity, the work of your faculties may be entirely beyond conscious estimation, and its results may not be seen or understood.

Contemplative prayer is a deep and simplified spiritual activity in which the mind and will rest in a unified and simple concentration upon God, turned to Him, intent upon Him and absorbed in His own light, with a simple gaze which is perfect adoration because it silently tells God that we have left everything else and desire even to leave our own selves for His sake, and that He alone is important to us, He alone is our desire and our life, and nothing else can give us any joy.

What you most need in this dark journey is an unfaltering trust in the Divine guidance, as well as the courage to risk everything for Him. In many ways the journey seems to be a foolish gamble. And you may well make many mistakes. You are thoroughly capable of deceiving yourself. Humility and docile submission to the guidance of a good Director will neutralize the effect of your own mistakes. Even your Director himself may not always be right. But you must trust in God, who "writes straight on crooked lines" and brings great good out of evil. What matters in the contemplative life is not for you or your Director to be always infallibly *right*, but for you to be heroically faithful to grace and to love. If God calls you to Him, then He implicitly promises you all the graces you need to reach Him. You must be blindly faithful to this promise.

34

The Wrong Flame

IN any degree of the spiritual life, and even where there is no spiritual life at all, it can happen that a man will feel himself caught up in an emotional religious ferment in which he overflows with sensible, and even sentimental movements of love for God and other people. If he is completely inexperienced he will get the idea that he is very holy because of the holy feelings that are teeming in his heart.

All these things mean very little or nothing at all. They are a kind of sensible intoxication produced by some pleasure or other, and there is only an accidental difference between them and the tears that children sometimes shed when they go to the movies.

In themselves these movements of passion are indifferent. They can be used for good or evil, and for beginners in the spiritual life they are generally necessary. But even a beginner would be foolish to depend on them, because sooner or later he will have to do without them. In fact, his spiritual life will not really begin until he has learned in some measure to get along without the stimulus of emotion.

Even when we enter into the contemplative life we still carry our passions and our sensible nature along with us like a store of unprotected gasoline. And sometimes the sparks that fly in the pure darkness of contemplation get into that fuel by accident and start a blaze in the emotions and the senses.

The whole spirit is rocked and reels in an explosion of drunken joy or a storm of compunction which may be good and healthy, but which is still more or less animal, even though the spark that started the fire may have had a supernatural origin.

This blaze flares up and burns out in a few moments, or a half an hour. Whilst it lasts, you taste an intense pleasure which is sometimes deceptively lofty. But this joy occasionally betrays itself by a certain heaviness that belongs to the sensual level and marks it for what it is: crude emotion. Sometimes it may even produce a good natural effect. A burst of spiritual exuberance can tone you up on a feast day, after weeks of struggle and labour. But generally the effect of this commotion is no better than natural. When it is all over you have no more profit than you might have got from a couple of glasses of champagne or a good swim. So to that extent it is a good thing.

But the danger is that you will attach the wrong kind of importance to these manifestations of religious emotion. Really they are not important at all, and although sometimes they are unavoidable, it does not seem prudent to desire them. And as a matter of fact, everyone who has received any kind of training in the interior life knows that it is not considered good sense to go after these consolations with too heavy an intensity of purpose. Nevertheless, many of those who seem to be so superior to the sensible element in religion show, by their devotions, their taste for sentimental pictures and sticky music and mushy spiritual reading, that their whole interior life is a concentrated campaign for "lights" and "consolations" and "tears of compunction," if not "interior words" with, perhaps, the faintly disguised hope of a vision or two and, eventually, the stigmata.

FOR anyone who is really called to infused contemplation this taste for "experience" can be one of the most dangerous obstacles in his interior life. It is the rock on which many who might have become contemplatives have ended in shipwreck. And it is all the more dangerous because even in the houses of contemplative orders people do not always clearly understand the difference between mystical contemplation in the proper sense and all these accidentals, these experiences, these manifestations and curiosities, which may or may not be supernatural, and which have no essential connection with sanctity or with the pure love which is at the heart of true contemplation.

THEREFORE the healthiest reaction to these outbursts is an obscure repugnance for the pleasures and the excitements they bring. You recognize that these things offer no real fruit and no lasting satisfaction. They tell you nothing reliable about God or about yourself. They give you no real strength, only the momentary illusion of holiness. And when you grow more experienced, how much they blind you and how capable they are of deceiving you and leading you astray.

You will try to withdraw from them and to avoid the occasions that bring them on, if you can tell what might be likely to bring them on. But you will not upset yourself by offering a violent resistance; it is enough to remain peacefully indifferent toward them.

And when there is nothing you can do to prevent these feelings of inebriation and spiritual joy you accept them with patience and with reserve and even with a certain humility and thankfulness, realizing that you would not suffer such excitements if there were not so much natural steam left in you. You withdraw your consent from anything that may be inordinate about them, and leave the rest to God, waiting for the hour of your deliverance into the real joys, the purely spiritual joys of a contemplation in which your nature and your emotions and your own self hood no longer run riot, but in which you are absorbed and immersed, not in this staggering drunkenness of the senses but in the clean, intensely pure intoxication of a spirit liberated in God.

Passion and emotion certainly have their place in the life of prayer—but they must be purified, ordered, brought into submission to the highest love. Then they too can share in the spirit's joy and even, in their own small way, contribute to it. But until they are spiritually mature the passions must be treated firmly and with reserve, even in the "consolations" of prayer. When are they spiritually mature? When they are pure, clean, gentle, quiet, nonviolent, forgetful of themselves, detached and above all when they are humble and obedient to reason and to grace.

35

Renunciation

THE way to contemplation is an obscurity so obscure that it is no longer even dramatic. There is nothing in it that can be grasped and cherished as heroic or even unusual. And so, for a contemplative, there is supreme value in the ordinary everyday routine of work, poverty, hardship and monotony that characterize the lives of all the poor, uninteresting and forgotten people in the world.

Christ, who came on earth to form contemplatives and teach men the ways of sanctity and prayer, could easily have surrounded Himself with ascetics who starved themselves to death and terrified the people with strange trances. But His Apostles were workmen, fishermen, publicans who made themselves conspicuous only by their disregard for most of the intricate network of devotions and ceremonial practices and moral gymnastics of the professionally holy.

The surest asceticism is the bitter insecurity and labour and nonentity of the really poor. To be utterly dependent on other people. To be ignored and despised and forgotten. To know little of respectability or comfort. To take orders and work hard for little or no money: it is a hard school, and one which most pious people do their best to avoid.

Nor are they to be entirely blamed. Misery as such, destitution as such, is not the way to contemplative union. I certainly don't mean that in order to be a saint one has to live in a slum, or that a contemplative monastery has to aim at reproducing the kind of life that is lived in tenements. It is not filth and hunger that make saints, nor even poverty itself, but love of poverty and love of the poor.

It is true, however, that a certain degree of economic security is morally necessary to provide a minimum of stability without which a life of prayer can hardly be learned. But "a certain degree of economic security" does not mean comfort, the satisfaction of every bodily and psychological need, and a high standard of living. The contemplative needs to be properly fed, clothed and housed. But he also needs to share something of the hardship of the poor. He needs to be able to identify himself honestly and sincerely with the poor, to be able to look at life through their eyes, and to do this because he is really one of them. This is not true unless to some extent he participates in the risk of poverty: that is to say, unless he has to do many jobs he would rather not do, suffer many inconveniences with patience, and be content with many things that could be a great deal better.

Many religious people, who say they love God, detest and fear the very thought of a poverty that is real enough to mean insecurity, hunger, dirt. And yet you will find men who go down and live among the poor not because they love God (in whom they do not believe) or even because they love the poor, but simply because they hate the rich and want to stir up the poor to hate the rich too. If men can suffer these things for the venomous pleasure of hatred, why do so few become poor out of love, in order both to find God in poverty and give Him to other men?

NEVERTHELESS it must not be thought that no man can become a contemplative unless his whole life is always externally miserable and disgusting. To live frugally and laboriously, depending on God and not on material things which we no longer have, and doing our best to get along with other people who do not, perhaps, treat us with uniform kindness and consideration, all this may add up to an atmosphere of peace and tranquillity and contentment and joy. There may even be a certain natural comeliness about it, and in fact the simplicity of a life of work and poverty can at times be more beautiful than the elaborate life of those who think their money can buy them beauty and surround them with pleasant things. Anybody who has been in the house of a French or Italian peasant knows that much.

Life in a Trappist monastery is fundamentally peasant life. The closer it conforms to the poverty and frugality and simplicity of those who have to dig their living out of the land, the more it fulfils its essential purpose, which is to dispose men for contemplation.

It is good for a monastery to be poor. It is good for the monks to have to be content with clothes that are worn very thin and covered with patches and to have to depend on their fields more than on Mass-stipends and the gifts of benefactors. However, there is a limit beyond which poverty in a monastery ought not to go. Destitution is not good for monks or for anybody else. You cannot be expected to lead the contemplative life if you are always ill, or starving to death and crushed by the physical struggle to keep body and soul together. And though it may be good for a monastery to be poor, the average monk will not prosper spiritually in a house where the poverty is really so desperate that everything else has to be sacrificed to manual labour and material cares.

It often happens that an old brother who has spent his life making cheese or baking bread or repairing shoes or driving a team of mules is a greater contemplative and more of a saint than a priest who has absorbed all Scripture and Theology and knows the writings of great saints and mystics and has had more time for meditation and contemplation and prayer.

But, although this may be quite true—and indeed it is so familiar that it has become a cliché—it must not make us forget that learning has an important part to play in the contemplative life. Nor should it make us forget that the work of the intellect, properly carried out, is itself a school of humility. The cliché about the "old brother making cheese" in contrast to the "proud intellectual priest" has often been used as an excuse to contemn and to evade the necessary effort of theological study. It is all very well to have many men in monasteries who are humbly dedicated to manual labour: but if they are also and at the same time learned men and theologians, this very fact may make their humility and their participation in manual work all the more significant.

Humility implies, first of all, a dedicated acceptance of one's duty in life. It is not humility for a priest who should know his theology to neglect study and render himself incapable of advising and guiding others, under the pretext of remaining humble and simple. Indeed, one sometimes finds in contemplatives a kind of pride in being unlearned, an intellectual snobbery turned inside out, a self-complacent contempt for theology, as if the mere fact of *not* knowing much of anything automatically raised one to the status of a contemplative.

Contemplation, far from being opposed to theology, is in fact the normal perfection of theology. We must not separate intellectual study of divinely revealed truth and contemplative experience of that truth as if they could never have anything to do with one another. On the contrary they are simply two aspects of the same thing. Dogmatic and mystical theology, or theology and "spirituality" are not to be set apart in mutually exclusive categories, as if mysticism were for saintly women and theological study were for practical but, alas, unsaintly men. This fallacious division perhaps explains much that is actually lacking both in theology and in spirituality. But the two belong together, just as body and soul belong together. Unless they are united, there is no fervour, no life and no spiritual value in theology, no substance, no meaning and no sure orientation in the contemplative life.

ONE of the first things to learn if you want to be a contemplative is how to mind your own business.

Nothing is more suspicious, in a man who seems holy, than an impatient desire to reform other men.

A serious obstacle to recollection is the mania for directing those you have not been appointed to direct, reforming those you have not been asked to reform, correcting those over whom you have no jurisdiction. How can you do these things and keep your mind at rest? Renounce this futile concern with other men's affairs!

Pay as little attention as you can to the faults of other people and none at all to their natural defects and eccentricities.

THE issue on which all sanctity depends is renunciation, detachment, self-denial. But self-denial does not end when we have given up all our deliberate faults and imperfections.

To keep yourself out of obvious sins; to avoid the things that are evidently wrong because they shame and degrade your nature; to perform acts that are universally respected because they are demanded by our very dignity as human beings: all that is not yet sanctity. To avoid sin and practise virtue is not to be a saint, it is only to be a man, a human being. This is only the beginning of what God wants of you. But it is a necessary beginning, because you cannot have supernatural perfection unless you have first (by God's grace) perfected your own nature on its own level. Before you can be a saint you have got to become human. An animal cannot be a contemplative.

However, it is relatively simple to get rid of faults that we recognize as faults—although that too can be terribly hard. But the crucial problem of perfection and interior purity is in the renunciation and uprooting of all our *unconscious* attachments to created things and to our own will and desires.

In fighting deliberate and evident vices a planned strategy of resolutions and penances is the best way—if not the only way. You plan your campaign and fight it out and reshape the plan according to the changes in the aspect of the battle. You pray and suffer and hang on and give things up and hope and sweat, and the varying contours of the struggle work out the shape of your liberty.

When it ends, and when you have a good habit to work with, do not forget the moments of the battle when you were wounded and disarmed and helpless. Do not forget that, for all your efforts, you only won because of God, who did the fighting in you.

But when it comes to fighting the deep and unconscious habits of attachment which we can hardly dig up and recognize, all our meditations, self-examinations, resolutions and planned campaigns may not only be ineffective but may even sometimes lend assistance to our enemies. Because it may easily happen that our resolutions are dictated by the vice we need to get rid of. And so the proud man resolves to fast more and punish his flesh more because he wants to make himself feel like an athlete: his fasts and disciplines are imposed on him by his own vanity, and they strengthen the thing in him that most needs to be killed.

When a man is virtuous enough to be able to delude himself that he is almost perfect, he may enter into a dangerous condition of blindness in which all his violent efforts finally

H

to grasp perfection strengthen his hidden imperfections and confirm him in his attachment to his own judgment and his own will.

IN getting the best of our secret attachments—ones which we cannot see because they are principles of spiritual blindness—our own initiative is almost always useless. We need to leave the initiative in the hands of God working in our souls either directly in the night of aridity and suffering, or through events and other men. This is where so many holy people break down and go to pieces. As soon as they reach the point where they can no longer see the way and guide themselves by their own light, they refuse to go any further. They have no confidence in anyone except themselves. Their faith is largely an emotional illusion. It is rooted in their feelings, in their physique, in their temperament. It is a kind of natural optimism that is stimulated by moral activity and warmed by the approval of other men. If people oppose it, this kind of faith still finds refuge in self-complacency.

But when the time comes to enter the darkness in which we are naked and helpless and alone; in which we see the insufficiency of our greatest strength and the hollowness of our strongest virtues, in which we have nothing of our own to rely on, and nothing in our nature to support us, and nothing in the world to guide us or give us light—then we find out whether or not we live by faith.

It is in this darkness, when there is nothing left in us that can please or comfort our own minds, when we seem to be useless and worthy of all contempt, when we seem to have failed, when we seem to be destroyed and devoured, it is then that the deep and secret selfishness that is too close for us to identify is stripped away from our souls. It is in this darkness that we find true liberty. It is in this abandonment that we are made strong. This is the night which empties us and makes us pure.

Do not look for rest in any pleasure, because you were not created for pleasure: you were created for spiritual JOY. And if you do not know the difference between pleasure and spiritual joy you have not yet begun to live.

Life in this world is full of pain. But pain, which is the contrary of pleasure, is not necessarily the contrary of happiness or of joy. Because spiritual joy flowers in the full expansion of freedom that reaches out without obstacle to its supreme object, fulfilling itself in the perfect activity of disinterested love for which it was created.

Pleasure, which is selfish, suffers from everything that deprives us of some good we want to savour for our own sakes. But unselfish joy suffers from nothing but selfishness. Pleasure is restrained and killed by pain and suffering. Spiritual joy ignores suffering or laughs at it or even exploits it to purify itself of its greatest obstacle, selfishness.

True joy is found in the perfect willing of what we were made to will: in the intense and supple and free movement of our will rejoicing in what is good not merely for us but in itself.

Sometimes pleasure can be the death of joy, and so the man who has tasted the true joy is suspicious of pleasure. But anyone who knows true joy is never afraid of pain because he knows that pain can serve him as another opportunity of asserting—and tasting—his liberty.

And yet do not think that joy turns pleasure inside out and seeks pleasure in pain: joy, in so far as it is true, is above pain and does not feel pain. And that is why it laughs at pain and rejoices in confounding pain. It is the conquest of suffering by disinterestedness, by unselfishness, by perfect love.

Pain cannot touch this highest joy—except to bring it an accidental increase of purity by asserting the soul's freedom from sense and emotion and self-love, and isolating our wills in a clean liberty beyond the level of suffering.

And so it is a very sad thing when contemplatives look for little more than pleasure in their contemplation. That means that they will waste time and exhaust themselves in harmful efforts to avoid aridity, difficulty and pain—as if these things were evils. They lose their peace. And seeking pleasure in their prayer they make themselves almost incapable of joy.

FICKLENESS and indecision are signs of self-love.

If you can never make up your mind what God wills for you, but are always veering from one opinion to another, from one practice to another, from one method to another, it may be an indication that you are trying to get around God's will and do your own with a quiet conscience.

As soon as God gets you in one monastery you want to be in another.

As soon as you taste one way of prayer, you want to try another. You are always making resolutions and breaking them by counter-resolutions. You ask your confessor and do not remember the answers. Before you finish one book you begin another, and with every book you read you change the whole plan of your interior life.

Soon you will have no interior life at all. Your whole existence will be a patchwork of confused desires and daydreams and velleities in which you do nothing except defeat the work of grace: for all this is an elaborate subconscious device of your nature to resist God, whose work in your soul demands the sacrifice of all that you desire and delight in, and, indeed, of all that you are.

So keep still, and let Him do some work.

This is what it means to renounce not only pleasures and possessions, but even your own self.

36

Inward Destitution

ONE of the greatest sufferings of a contemplative is to feel the terrible, inescapable coarseness and grossness and inadequacy of the highest human modes of love and intellection when they are seen in the light of God, when they reach out towards God and fail.

Measure, if you can, the sorrow of realizing that you have a nature destined by God for the gift of a beatitude which utterly transcends everything that you are and can ever be; of finding yourself left with nothing but yourself; of finding yourself without the gift which is the only meaning of your existence. Then the highest perfection of natural life, of human understanding, the purest and finest tension of the human will reaching out in desire for everything that is perfect, appears to you as something essentially vulgar and worthless. Even without your mistakes and your sins, everything that you are or can be or can possess appears to you as if it were nothing, because it has no power to procure for you the immense gift which is utterly beyond you and which is the only real reason why you were created.

But when, on top of all that, you see that your nature is still twisted and disfigured by selfishness and by the disorder of sin, and that you are cramped and warped by a way of living that turns you incessantly back upon your own pleasure and your own interest, and that you cannot escape this distortion: that you cannot even deserve to escape it, by your own power, what will your sorrow be? This is the root of what the saints called compunction: the grief, the anguish of being helpless to be anything but what you were not meant to be.

Then, in prayer, all sweetness becomes a sickness. Consolation repels you because the smallest taste of it brings surfeit. All light brings pain to the mind by its insufficiency. Your will no longer seems able to dare to act. The slightest movement reminds it of its uselessness, and it dies of shame.

And yet, strangely, it is in this helplessness that we come upon the beginning of joy. We discover that as long as we stay still the pain is not so bad and there is even a certain peace, a certain richness, a certain strength, a certain companionship that makes itself present to us when we are beaten down and lie flat with our mouths in the dust, hoping for hope.

Then, as peace settles upon the soul and we accept what we are and what we are not, we begin to realize that this great poverty is our greatest fortune. For when we are stripped of the riches that were not ours and could not possibly endow us with anything but trouble, when we rest even from that good and licit activity of knowing and desiring which still could not give us any possession of our true end and happiness, then we become aware that the whole meaning of our life is a poverty and emptiness which, far from being a defeat, are really the pledge of all the great supernatural gifts of which they are a potency.

We become like vessels that have been emptied of water that they may be filled with wine. We are like glass cleansed of dust and grime to receive the sun and vanish into its light.

Once we begin to find this emptiness, no poverty is poor enough, no emptiness is empty enough, no humility lowers us enough for our desires.

Then our greatest sorrow is to find that we still attach importance to ourselves, still can be great in our own eyes, for we have begun to know that any shadow cast upon the transparency of a pure and empty soul is an illusion and an obstacle to the unadulterated light of God. And we see that our knowledge is darkness by comparison with His light. Power is supreme weakness and makes us incapable of His strength, and all human desire deceives and disturbs us and turns us away from Him.

The more our faculties are emptied of their desire and their tension towards created things, and the more they collect themselves into peace and interior silence and reach into the darkness where God is present to their deepest hunger, the more they feel a pure, burning impatience to be free and rid of all the last obstacles and attachments that still stand between them and the emptiness that will be capable of being filled with God.

It is then that the monk suddenly discovers the great value of even the simplest and most fundamental means of renunciation which his rule may offer him. His attitude towards all the things that are called penances begins to change. Before, he nerved himself for them with a kind of athletic tension, and depended much on the moral support of others doing the same thing, fasting and working and praying along with him. Now he turns to these hard and obscure and plain ways of penance because they give rest to his soul, they pacify him; yet it is not because he conceives them as cleansing and perfecting his own heart that he seeks these means: he rests in them because he can no longer rest in anything that is his own will. His peace is in the will of another. His freedom is found in dependence upon God through another.

And it is the truly contemplative man who is nourished by obedience and finds his peace in the simplicity of a child or of a novice. Yet that comparison too is very misleading. A mature contemplative is far more simple than any child or any novice, because theirs is a more or less negative simplicity—the simplicity of those in whom potential complications have not yet had a chance to develop. But in the contemplative, all complexities have now begun to straighten themselves out and dissolve into unity and emptiness and interior peace.

THE contemplative, nourished by emptiness, endowed by poverty and liberated from all sorrow by simple obedience, drinks fortitude and joy from the will of God in all things.

Without any need for complicated reasoning or mental efforts or special acts, his life is a prolonged immersion in the rivers of tranquillity that flow from God into the whole universe and draw all things back into God.

For God's love is like a river springing up in the depth of the Divine Substance and flowing endlessly through His creation, filling all things with life and goodness and strength.

All things, except our own sins, are carried and come to us in the waters of this pure and irresistible stream.

If we accept them in tranquillity, submitting to the pressure of the waters by a clean and unquestioning faith and a love perfect and detached from all resistance, God's will enters into the depths of our own freedom and carries our lives and all our acts and desires away on the tide of His own joy. True peace is only found by those who have learned to ride and swim with the strong current of this stream. For them life becomes simple and easy. Every moment is rich in happiness. All events are intelligible, if not in their details at least in their relation to the great wholeness of life.

But if we refuse to accept His will (and this is sin) we are nevertheless overwhelmed by the flood which no power can resist.

All sorrow, hardship, difficulty, struggle, pain, unhappiness, and ultimately death itself can be traced to rebellion against God's love for us.

WHEN the Gift of Understanding has opened our eyes in contemplation, we ought not to disturb God, in our souls, by the noise of our own temporal activity. We should receive His light in silence, tranquillity and deep thankfulness, realizing that at this moment the highest praise we can offer Him is to sacrifice every attempt to praise Him in human language and resist the temptation to reduce Him to the level of our own concepts and understandings. Not that our words cannot praise Him: but they can only praise Him on our own level. We would have to withdraw from Him and emerge from His depths before words and ideas could separate themselves out and take shape in our minds. For in the depths of contemplative prayer there seems to be no division between subject and object, and there is no reason to make any statement either about God or about oneself. He IS and this reality absorbs everything else.

So it is great praise of God to remain in His silence and darkness and when we have received this gift from Him it would be poor thanks indeed to prefer our own dim light and desire some feeling of Him that would give us some false and human sense of His being.

37

Sharing the Fruits of Contemplation

WE do not see God in contemplation—we *know* Him by love: for He is pure Love and when we taste the experience of loving God for His own sake alone, we know by experience Who and what He is.

True mystical experience of God and supreme renunciation of everything outside of God coincide. They are two aspects of the same thing. For when our minds and wills are perfectly free from every created attachment, they are immediately filled with the gift of God's love: not because things necessarily have to happen that way, but because this is His will, the gift of His love to us. "Everyone who has left his home or his father, or his mother, or his wife for my sake shall receive a hundredfold and shall possess eternal life."

We experience God in proportion as we are stripped and emptied of attachment to His creatures. And when we have been delivered from every other desire we shall taste the perfection of an incorruptible joy.

God does not give His joy to us for ourselves alone, and if we could possess Him for ourselves alone we would not possess Him at all. Any joy that does not overflow from our souls and help other men to rejoice in God does not come to us from God. (But do not think that you have to see how it overflows into the souls of others. In the economy of His grace, you may be sharing His gifts with someone you will never know until you get to heaven.)

IF we experience God in contemplation, we experience Him not for ourselves alone but also for others.

Yet if our experience of God comes from God, one of the signs may be a great diffidence in telling others about it. To speak about the gift He has given us would seem to dissipate it and leave a stain on the pure emptiness where God's light shone. No one is more shy than a contemplative about his contemplation. Sometimes it gives him almost physical pain to speak to anyone of what he has seen of God. Or at least it is intolerable for him to speak about it as his own experience.

At the same time he most earnestly wants everybody else to share his peace and his joy. His contemplation gives him a new outlook on the world of men. He looks about him with a secret and tranquil surmise which he perhaps admits to no one, hoping to find in the faces of other men or to hear in their voices some sign of vocation and potentiality for the same deep happiness and wisdom.

He finds himself speaking of God to the men in whom he hopes he has recognized the light of his own peace, the awakening of his own secret: or if he cannot speak to them, he writes for them, and his contemplative life is still imperfect without sharing, without companionship, without communion.

AT no time in the spiritual life is it more necessary to be completely docile and subject to the most delicate movements of God's will and His grace than when you try to share the knowledge of His love with other men. It is much better to be so diffident that you risk not sharing it with them at all, than to throw it all away by trying to give it to other people before you have received it yourself. The contemplative who tries to preach contemplation before he himself really knows what it is, will prevent both himself and others from finding the true path to God's peace.

In the first place he will substitute his own natural enthusiasm and imagination and poetry for the reality of the light that is in him, and he will become absorbed in the business of communicating something that is practically incommunicable: and although there is some benefit in this even for his own soul (for it is a kind of meditation on the interior life and on God) still he runs the risk of being drawn away from the simple light and silence in which God is known without words and concepts, and losing himself in reasoning and language and metaphor.

The highest vocation in the Kingdom of God is that of sharing one's contemplation with others and bringing other men to the experimental knowledge of God that is given to those who love Him perfectly. But the possibility of mistake and error is just as great as the vocation itself.

In the first place the mere fact that you have discovered something of contemplation does not yet mean that you are supposed to pass it on to somebody else. The sharing of contemplation with others implies two vocations: one to be a contemplative, and another still to teach contemplation. Both of them have to be verified.

But then, as soon as you think of yourself as teaching contemplation to others, you make another mistake. No one teaches contemplation except God, who gives it. The best you can do is write something or say something that will serve as an occasion for someone else to realize what God wants of him.

ONE of the worst things about an ill-timed effort to share the knowledge of contemplation with other people is that you assume that everybody else will want to see things from your own point of view when, as a matter of fact, they will not. They will raise objections to everything that you say, and you will find yourself in a theological controversy—or worse, a pseudo-scientific one—and nothing is more useless for a contemplative than controversy. There is no point whatever in trying to make people with a different vocation get excited about the kind of interior life that means so much to you. And if they are called to contemplation, a long, involved argument full of technicalities and abstract principles is not the thing that will help them to get there.

Those who are too quick to think they must go out and share their contemplation with other men tend to ruin their own contemplation and give false notions of it to others, by trusting too much in words and language and discourse to do the work that can only be accomplished in the depths of man's soul by the infused light of God.

Often we will do much more to make men contemplatives by leaving them alone and minding our own business—which is contemplation itself—than by breaking in on them with what we think we know about the interior life. For when we are united with God in silence and darkness and when our faculties are raised above the level of their own natural activity, and rest in the pure, tranquil, incomprehensible cloud that surrounds the presence of God, our prayer and the grace that is given to us tend of their very nature to overflow invisibly through the Mystical Body of Christ, and we who dwell together invisibly in the bond of the One Spirit of God affect one another more than we can ever realize by our own union with God, by our spiritual vitality in Him.

One who has a very little of this prayer, the mere beginning of contemplation, and who scarcely even realizes anything of what he has, can do immense things for the souls of other men simply by keeping himself quietly attentive to the obscure presence of God, about which he could not possibly hope to formulate an intelligible sentence. And if he did try to start talking about it and reasoning about it, he would at once lose the little that he had of it and would help no one, least of all himself.

Therefore the best way to prepare ourselves for the possible vocation of sharing contemplation with other men is not to study how to talk and reason about contemplation, but to withdraw ourselves as much as we can from talk and argument and retire into silence and humility of heart in which God will purify our love of all its human imperfections. Then in His own time He will set our hand to the work He wants us to do, and we will find ourselves doing it without being quite able to realize how we got there, or how it all started. And by that time the work will not absorb us in a way that will disturb our minds. We will be able to keep our tranquillity and our freedom, and above all we will learn to leave the results to God, and not to indulge our own vanity by insisting on quick and visible conversions in everyone we talk to.

Perhaps it looks easy on paper, and perhaps it would really be easy if we were altogether simple and made no difficulties about letting God work in us and through us. But in actual practice one of the last barricades of egoism, and one which many saints have refused to give up entirely, is this insistence on doing the work and getting the results and enjoying them *ourselves*. We are the ones who want to carry off the glory for the work done. And perhaps that was why some saints did not get to the highest contemplation: they wanted to *do* too much for themselves. And God let them get away with it.

And therefore although contemplation, like all good things, demands to be shared and will only be perfectly enjoyed and possessed by each one of us when it is possessed in common by all who are called to it, we must not forget that this perfect communion belongs only to heaven.

Be careful, then, of assuming that because you like certain people and are naturally inclined to choose them for your friends and share with them your natural interests, that they are also called to be contemplatives and that you must teach them all how to become so. The aptitude may or may not be there. Perhaps there is a strong likelihood that it *is* there: but if it is, be content to let God take care of its development in them. Be glad if He uses you as an occasion or as an instrument, but be careful not to get in His way with your own innate instinct for companionship. For in this world it is not good to be too eager for the achievement of any, even of the best of ends; and one who knows by experience that God is always present everywhere and always ready to make Himself known to those who love Him, will not quickly prefer the uncertain value of human activity to the tranquillity and certitude of this infinite and all-important possession.

38

Pure Love

SO far, though not explicitly dividing them, we have spoken about three modes of contemplation. They are three possible beginnings.

1. The best of these kinds of beginnings is a sudden emptying of the soul in which images vanish, concepts and words are silent, and freedom and clarity suddenly open out within you until your whole being embraces the wonder, the depth, the obviousness and yet the emptiness and unfathomable incomprehensibility of God. This touch, this clean breath of understanding comes relatively rarely. The two other beginnings can be habitual states.

2. The most usual entrance to contemplation is through a desert of aridity in which, although you see nothing and feel nothing and apprehend nothing and are conscious only of a certain interior suffering and anxiety, yet you are drawn and held in this darkness and dryness because it is the only place in which you can find any kind of stability and peace. As you progress, you learn to rest in this arid quietude, and the assurance of a comforting and mighty presence at the heart of this experience grows on you more and more, until you gradually realize that it is God revealing Himself to you in a light that is painful to your nature and to all its faculties, because it is infinitely above them and because its purity is at war with your own selfishness and darkness and imperfection.

3. Then there is a *quietud sabrosa*, a tranquillity full of savour and rest and unction in which, although there is nothing to feed

and satisfy either the senses or the imagination or the intellect, the will rests in a deep, luminous and absorbing experience of love. This love is like the shining cloud that enveloped the Apostles on Thabor so that they exclaimed: "Lord, it is good for us to be here!" And from the depths of this cloud come touches of reassurance, the voice of God speaking without words, uttering His own Word. For you recognize, at least in some obscure fashion, that this beautiful, deep, meaningful tranquillity that floods your whole being with its truth and its substantial peace has something to do with the Mission of the Second Person in your soul, is an accompaniment and sign of that mission.

Thus, to many, the cloud of their contemplation becomes identified in a secret way with the Divinity of Christ and also with His Heart's love for us, so that their contemplation itself becomes the presence of Christ, and they are absorbed in a suave and pure communion with Christ. And this tranquillity is learned most of all in Eucharistic Communion.

He becomes to them a sensible presence who follows them and envelops them wherever they go and in all that they do, a pillar of cloud by day and a pillar of fire in the night, and when they have to be absorbed in some distracting work, they nevertheless easily find God again by a quick glance into their own souls. And sometimes when they do not think to return to the depths and rest in Him, He nevertheless draws them unexpectedly into His obscurity and peace, or invades them from within themselves with a tide of quiet, unutterable joy.

Sometimes these tides of joy are concentrated into strong touches, contacts of God that wake the soul with a bound of wonder and delight, a flash of flame that blazes like an exclamation of inexpressible happiness and sometimes burns with a wound that is delectable although it gives pain. God cannot touch many with this flame, or touch even these heavily. But nevertheless it seems that these deep movements of the Spirit of His Love keep striving, at least lightly, to impress themselves on every one that God draws into this happy and tranquil light.

IN all these three beginnings you remain aware of yourself as being on the threshold of something more or less indefinite. In the second you are scarcely conscious of it at all: you only have a vague, unutterable sense that peace underlies the darkness and aridity in which you find yourself. You scarcely dare admit it to yourself, but in spite of all your misgivings you realize that you are going somewhere and that your journey is guided and directed and that you can feel safe.

In the third you are in the presence of a more definite and more personal Love, who invades your mind and will in a way you cannot grasp, eluding every attempt on your part to contain and hold Him by any movement of your own soul. You know that this "Presence" is God. But for the rest He is hidden in a cloud, although He is so near as to be inside you and outside you and all around you.

When this contact with God deepens and becomes more pure, the cloud thins. In proportion as the cloud gets less opaque, the experience of God opens out inside you as a terrific emptiness. What you experience is the emptiness and purity of your own faculties, produced in you by a created effect of God's love. Nevertheless, since it is God Himself who directly produces this effect and makes Himself known by it, without any other intermediary, the experience is more than purely subjective and does tell you something about God that you cannot know in any other way.

These effects are intensified by the light of understanding, infused into your soul by the Spirit of God and raising it suddenly into an atmosphere of dark, breathless clarity in which God, though completely defeating and baffling all your natural understanding, becomes somehow obvious.

However, in all these things you remain very far from God, much farther than you realize. And there are always two of you. There is yourself and there is God making Himself known to you by these effects.

BUT as long as there is this sense of separation, this awareness of distance and difference between ourselves and God, we have not entered into the fullness of contemplation.

As long as there is an "I" that is the definite subject of a contemplative experience, an "I" that is aware of itself and of its contemplation, an "I" that can possess a certain "degree of spirituality," then we have not yet passed over the Red Sea, we have not yet "gone out of Egypt." We remain in the realm of multiplicity, activity, incompleteness, striving and desire. The true inner self, the true indestructible and immortal person, the true "I" who answers to a new and secret name known only to himself and to God, does not "have" anything, even "contemplation." This "I" is not the kind of subject that can amass experiences, reflect on them, reflect on himself, for this "I" is not the superficial and empirical self that we know in our everyday life.

It is a great mistake to confuse the *person* (the spiritual and hidden self, united with God) and the *ego*, the exterior, empirical self, the psychological individuality who forms a kind of mask for the inner and hidden self. This outer self is nothing but an evanescent shadow. Its biography and its existence both end together at death. Of the inmost self, there is neither biography nor end. The outward self can "have" much, "enjoy" much, "accomplish" much, but in the end all its possessions, joys and accomplishments are nothing, and the outer self is, itself, nothing: a shadow, a garment that is cast off and consumed by decay.

It is another mistake to identify the outer self with the body and the inner self with the soul. This is an understandable mistake, but it is very misleading because after all body and soul are incomplete substances, parts of one whole being: and the inner self is not a *part* of us, it is all of us. It is our *whole reality*. Whatever is added to it is fortuitous, transient, and inconsequential. Hence both body and soul belong to, or better, subsist in our real self, the person that we are. The *ego*, on the other hand, is a self-constructed illusion that "has" our body and part of our soul at its disposal because it has "taken over" the functions of the inner self, as a result of what we call man's "fall." That is precisely one of the main effects of the fall: that man has become alienated from his inner self which is the image of God. Man has been turned, spiritually, inside out, so that his *ego* plays the part of the "person"—a role which it actually has no right to assume.

In returning to God and to ourselves, we have to begin with what we actually are. We have to start from our alienated condition. We are prodigals in a distant country, the "region of unlikeness," and we must seem to travel far in that region before we seem to reach our own land (and yet secretly we are in our own land all the time!). The "ego," the "outer self," is respected by God and allowed to carry out the function which our inner self cannot yet assume on its own. We have to act, in our everyday life, as if we were what our outer self indicates us to be. But at the same time we must remember that we are *not* entirely what we seem to be, and that what appears to be our "self" is soon going to disappear into nothingness.

One of the most widespread errors of our time is a super-ficial "personalism" which identifies the "person" with the external self, the empirical ego, and devotes itself solemnly to the cultivation of this ego.

But this is the cult of a pure illusion, the illusion of what is popularly imagined to be "personality" or, worse still, "dynamic" and "successful" personality. When this error is taken over into religion it leads to the worst kind of nonsense—a cult of psychologism and self-expression which vitiates our whole cultural and spiritual self. Our reality, our true self, is hidden in what appears to us to be nothingness and void. What we are not seems to be real, what we are seems to be unreal. We can rise above this unreality, and recover our hidden identity. And that is why the way to reality is the way of humility which brings us to reject the illusory self and accept the "empty" self that is "nothing" in our own eyes and in the eyes of men, but is our true reality in the eyes of God: for this reality is "in God" and "with Him" and belongs entirely to Him. Yet of course it is ontologically distinct from Him, and in no sense part of the divine nature or absorbed in that nature.

This inmost self is beyond the kind of experience which says "I want," "I love," "I know," "I feel." It has its own way of knowing, loving and experiencing which is a divine way and not a human one, a way of identity, of union, of "espousal," in which there is no longer a separate psychological individuality drawing all good and all truth towards itself, and thus loving and knowing for itself. Lover and Beloved are "one spirit."

Therefore, as long as we experience ourselves in prayer as an "I" standing on the threshold of the abyss of purity and emptiness that is God, waiting to "receive something" from Him, we are still far from the most intimate and secret unitive knowledge that is pure contemplation.

From our side of the threshold this darkness, this emptiness, look deep and vast—and exciting. There is nothing we can do about entering in. We cannot force our way over the edge, although there is no barrier.

But the reason is perhaps that there is also no abyss.

There you remain, somehow feeling that the next step will be a plunge and you will find yourself flying in interstellar space.

When the next step comes, you do not take the step, you do not know the transition, you do not fall into anything. You do not go anywhere, and so you do not know the way by which you got there or the way by which you come back afterwards. You are certainly not lost. You do not fly. There is no space, or there is all space: it makes no difference.

The next step is not a step.

You are not transported from one degree to another.

What happens is that the separate entity that is *you* apparently disappears and nothing seems to be left but a pure freedom indistinguishable from infinite Freedom, love identified with Love. Not two loves, one waiting for the other, striving for the other, seeking for the other, but Love Loving in Freedom.

Would you call this experience? I think you might say that this only becomes an experience in a man's memory. Otherwise it seems wrong even to speak of it as something that happens. Because things that happen have to happen to some subject, and experiences have to be experienced by someone. But here the subject of any divided or limited or creature experience seems to have vanished. You are not you, you are fruition. If you like, you do not have an experience, you become Experience: but that is entirely different, because you no longer exist in such a way that you can reflect on yourself or see yourself having an experience, or judge what is going on, if it can be said that something is going on that is not eternal and unchanging and an activity so tremendous that it is infinitely still.

And here all adjectives fall to pieces. Words become stupid. Everything you say is misleading—unless you list every possible experience and say: "*That is not what it is.*" "*That is not what I am talking about.*"

Metaphor has now become hopeless altogether. Talk about "darkness" if you must: but the thought of darkness is already too dense and too coarse. Anyway, it is no longer darkness. You can speak of "emptiness" but that makes you think of floating around in space: and this is nothing spatial.

What it is, is freedom. It is perfect love. It is pure renunciation. It is the fruition of God.

It is not freedom inhering in some subject; it is not love as an action dominated by an impulse germane to one's own being; it is not renunciation that plans and executes itself after the manner of a virtue.

It is freedom living and circulating in God, who is Freedom. It is love loving in Love. It is the purity of God rejoicing in His own liberty.

And here, where contemplation becomes what it is really meant to be, it is no longer something infused by God into a created subject, so much as God living in God and identifying a created life with His own Life so that there is nothing left of any significance but God living in God.

If a man who had thus been vindicated and delivered and fulfilled and destroyed could think and speak at all it would certainly never be to think and speak of himself as someone separate, or as the subject of a grandiose experience.

And that is why it does not really make much sense to speak of all this as the high point of a series of degrees, and as something great by comparison with other experiences which are less great. It is outside the limit within which comparisons have meaning. It is beyond the level of "ways" that correspond to any of our notions of travel, beyond the degrees that correspond to our ideas of a progression.

Yet this too is a beginning. It is the lowest level in a new order in which all the levels are immeasurable and unthinkable. It is not yet the perfection of the interior life.

THE most important thing that remains to be said about this perfect contemplation in which the soul vanishes out of itself by the perfect renunciation of all desires and all things, is that it can have nothing to do with our ideas of greatness and exaltation, and is not therefore something which is subject to the sin of pride.

In fact, this perfect contemplation implies, by its very essence, the perfection of all humility. Pride is incompatible with it in every possible way. It is only something that a man could be proud of, or desire inordinately, or in some other way make material for sin, when it is completely misunderstood and taken for something which it is not and cannot be.

For pride, which is the inordinate attribution of goods and values and glories to one's own contingent and exterior self, cannot exist where one is incapable of reflecting on a separate "self" living apart from God.

How can a man be proud of anything when he is no longer able to reflect upon himself or realize himself or know himself? Morally speaking he is annihilated, because the source and agent and term of all his acts is God. And the essence of this contemplation is the pure and eternal joy that is in God because God is God: the serene and interminable exultation in the truth that He who is Perfect is infinitely Perfect, is Perfection.

To think that a man could be proud of this joy, once it had discovered him and delivered him, would be like saying: "This man is proud because the air is free." "This other man is proud because the sea is wet." "And here is one who is proud because the mountains are high and the snow on their summits is clean and the wind blows on the snow and makes a plume of cloud trail away from the high peaks."

Here is a man who is dead and buried and gone and his memory has vanished from the world of men and he no longer exists among the living who wander about in time: and will you call him proud because the sunlight fills the huge arc of sky over the country where he lived and died and was buried, back in the days when he existed?

So it is with one who has vanished into God by pure contemplation. God alone is left. He is the "I" who acts there. He is the one who loves and knows and rejoices.

Can God be proud, or can God sin?

Suppose such a man were once in his life to vanish into God for the space of a minute.

All the rest of his life has been spent in sins and virtues, in good and evil, in labour and struggle, in sickness and health, in gifts, in sorrows, in achieving and regretting, in planning and hoping, in love and fear. He has seen things, considered them, known them; made judgments; spoken; acted wisely or not. He has blundered in and out of the contemplation of beginners. He has found the cloud, the obscure sweetness of God. He has known rest in prayer.

In all these things his life has been a welter of uncertainties. In the best of them he may have sinned. In his imperfect contemplation he may have found sin.

But in the moment of time, the minute, the little minute in which he was delivered into God (if he truly was so delivered) there is no question that then his life was pure; that then he gave glory to God; that then he did not sin; that in that moment of pure love he could not sin.

Can such union with God be the object of inordinate desire? Not if you understand it. Because you cannot inordinately desire

God to be God. You cannot inordinately desire that God's will be done for His own sake. But it is in these two desires perfectly conceived and fulfilled that we are emptied into Him and transformed into His joy and it is in these that we cannot sin.

It is in this ecstasy of pure love that we arrive at a true fulfilment of the First Commandment, loving God with our whole heart and our whole mind and all our strength. Therefore it is something that all men who desire to please God ought to desire —not for a minute, nor for half an hour, but for ever. It is in these souls that peace is established in the world.

They are the strength of the world, because they are the tabernacles of God in the world. They are the ones who keep the universe from being destroyed. They are the little ones. They do not know themselves. The whole earth depends on them. Nobody seems to realize it. These are the ones for whom it was all created in the first place. They shall inherit the land.

They are the only ones who will ever be able to enjoy life altogether. They have renounced the whole world and it has been given into their possession. They alone appreciate the world and the things that are in it. They are the only ones capable of understanding joy. Everybody else is too weak for joy. Joy would kill anybody but these meek. They are the clean of heart. They see God. He does their will, because His will is their own. He does all that they want, because He is the One who desires all their desires. They are the only ones who have everything that they can desire. Their freedom is without limit. They reach out for us to comprehend our misery and drown it in the tremendous expansion of their own innocence, that washes the world with its light.

Come, let us go into the body of that light. Let us live in the cleanliness of that song. Let us throw off the pieces of the world like clothing and enter naked into wisdom. For this is what all hearts pray for when they cry: "Thy will be done."

39

The General Dance

THE Lord made His world not in order to judge it, not in order merely to dominate it, to make it obey the dictates of an inscrutable and all-powerful will, not in order to find pleasure or displeasure in the way it worked: such was not the reason for creation either of the world or of man.

The Lord made the world and made man in order that He Himself might descend into the world, that He Himself might become Man. When He regarded the world He was about to make He saw His wisdom, as a man-child, "playing in the world, playing before Him at all times." And He reflected, "My delights are to be with the children of men."

The world was not made as a prison for fallen spirits who were rejected by God: this is the gnostic error. The world was made as a temple, a paradise, into which God Himself would descend to dwell familiarly with the spirits He had placed there to tend it for Him.

The early chapters of Genesis (far from being a pseudo-scientific account of the way the world was supposed to have come into being) are precisely a poetic and symbolic revelation, a completely *true*, though not literal, revelation of God's view of the universe and of His intentions for man. The point of these beautiful chapters is that God made the world as a garden in which He Himself took delight. He made man and gave to man the task of sharing in His own divine care for created things. He made man in His own image and likeness, as an artist, a worker, *homo faber*, as the gardener of paradise.

He let man decide for himself how created things were to be interpreted, understood and used: for Adam gave the animals their names (God gave them no names at all) and what names Adam gave them, that they were. Thus in his intelligence man, by the act of knowing, imitated something of the creative love of God for creatures. While the love of God, looking upon things, brought them into being, the love of man, looking upon things, reproduced the divine idea, the divine truth, in man's own spirit.

As God creates things by seeing them in His own Logos, man brings truth to life in his mind by the marriage of the divine light, in the being of the object, with the divine light in his own reason. The meeting of these two lights in one mind is truth.

But there is a higher light still, not the light by which man "gives names" and forms concepts, with the aid of the active intelligence, but the dark light in which no names are given, in which God confronts man not through the medium of things, but in His own simplicity. The union of the simple light of God with the simple light of man's spirit, in love, is contemplation. The two simplicities are one. They form, as it were, an emptiness in which there is no addition but rather the taking away of names, of forms, of content, of subject matter, of identities. In this meeting there is not so much a fusion of identities as a disappearance of identities. The Bible speaks of this very simply: "In the breeze after noon God came to walk with Adam in paradise." It is after noon, in the declining light of created day. In the free emptiness of the breeze that blows from where it pleases and goes where no one can estimate, God and man are together, not speaking in words, or syllables or forms. And that was the meaning of creation and of Paradise. But there was more.

The Word of God Himself was the "firstborn of every

creature." He "in whom all things consist" was not only to walk with man in the breeze after noon, but would also become man, and dwell with man as a brother.

The Lord would not only love His creation as a Father, but He would enter into His creation, emptying Himself, hiding Himself, as if He were not God but a creature. Why should He do this? Because He loved His creatures, and because He could not bear that His creatures should merely adore Him as distant, remote, transcendent and all-powerful. This was not the glory that He sought, for if He were merely adored as great, His creatures would in their turn make themselves great and lord it over one another. For where there is a great God, then there are also god-like men, who make themselves kings and masters. And if God were merely a great artist who took pride in His creation, then men too would build cities and palaces and exploit other men for their own glory. This is the meaning of the myth of Babel, and of the tower builders who would be "as gods" with their hanging gardens, and with the heads of their enemies hanging in the gardens. For they would point to God and say: "He too is a great builder, and has destroyed all His enemies."

(GOD said: I do not laugh at my enemies, because I wish to make it impossible for anyone to be my enemy. Therefore I identify myself with my enemy's own secret self.)

So God became man. He took on the weakness and ordinariness of man, and He hid Himself, becoming an anonymous and unimportant man in a very unimportant place. And He refused at any time to lord it over men, or to be a King, or to be a Leader, or to be a Reformer, or to be in any way superior to His own creatures. He would be nothing else but their brother, and their counsellor, and their servant, and their friend. He was in no accepted human sense an important person, though since that time we have made Him The Most Important Person. That is another matter: for though it is quite true that He is the King and Lord of all, the conqueror of death, the judge of the living and of the dead, the *Pantokrator*, yet He is also still the Son of Man, the hidden one, unknown, unremarkable, vulnerable. He can be killed. And when the Son of Man was put to death, He rose again from the dead, and was again with us, for He said: "Kill me, it does not matter."

Having died, He dies no more in His own Person. But because He became man and united man's nature to Himself, and died for man, and rose as man from the dead, He brought it about that the sufferings of all men became His own sufferings; their weakness and defencelessness became His weakness and defencelessness; their insignificance became His. But at the same time His own power, immortality, glory and happiness were given to them and could become theirs. So if the God-Man is still great, it is rather for our sakes than for His own that He wishes to be great and strong. For to Him, strength and weakness, life and death are dualities with which He is not concerned, being above them in His transcendent unity. Yet He would raise us also above these dualities by making us one with Him. For though evil and death can touch the evanescent, outer self in which we dwell estranged from Him, in which we are alienated and exiled in unreality, it can never touch the real inner self in which we have been made one with Him. For in becoming man, God became not only Jesus Christ but also potentially every man and woman that ever existed. In Christ, God became not only "this" man, but also in a broader and more mystical sense, yet no less truly, "every man."

THE presence of God in His world as its Creator depends on

no one but Him. His presence in the world as Man depends, in some measure, upon men. Not that we can do anything to change the mystery of the Incarnation in itself: but we are able to decide whether we ourselves, and that portion of the world which is ours, shall become *aware* of His presence, consecrated by it, and transfigured in its light.

We have the choice of two identities: the external mask which seems to be real and which lives by a shadowy autonomy for the brief moment of earthly existence, and the hidden, inner person who seems to us to be nothing, but who can give himself eternally to the truth in whom he subsists. It is this inner self that is taken up into the mystery of Christ, by His love, by the Holy Spirit, so that in secret we live "in Christ."

YET we must not deal in too negative a fashion even with the "external self." This self is not by nature evil, and the fact that it is unsubstantial is not to be imputed to it as some kind of crime. It is afflicted with metaphysical poverty: but all that is poor deserves mercy. So too our outward self: as long as it does not isolate itself in a lie, it is blessed by the mercy and the love of Christ. Appearances are to be accepted for what they are. The accidents of a poor and transient existence have, nevertheless, an ineffable value. They can be transparent media in which we apprehend the presence of God in the world. It is possible to speak of the exterior self as a mask: to do so is not necessarily to reprove it. The mask that each man wears may well be a disguise not only for that man's inner self but for God, wandering as a pilgrim and exile in His own creation.

And indeed, if Christ became man, it is because He wanted to be any man and every man. If we believe in the Incarnation of the Son of God, there should be no one on earth in whom we are not prepared to see, in mystery, the presence of Christ.

WHAT is serious to men is often very trivial in the sight of God. What in God might appear to us as "play" is perhaps what He Himself takes most seriously. At any rate the Lord plays and diverts Himself in the garden of His creation, and if we could let go of our own obsession with what we think is the meaning of it all, we might be able to hear His call and follow Him in His mysterious, cosmic dance. We do not have to go very far to catch echoes of that game, and of that dancing. When we are alone on a starlit night; when by chance we see the migrating birds in autumn descending on a grove of junipers to rest and eat; when we see children in a moment when they are really children; when we know love in our own hearts; or when, like the Japanese poet Bashō, we hear an old frog land in a quiet pond with a solitary splash—at such times the awakening, the turning inside out of all values, the "newness," the emptiness and the purity of vision that make themselves evident, provide a glimpse of the cosmic dance.

For the world and time are the dance of the Lord in emptiness. The silence of the spheres is the music of a wedding feast. The more we persist in misunderstanding the phenomena of life, the more we analyse them out into strange finalities and complex purposes of our own, the more we involve ourselves in sadness, absurdity and despair. But it does not matter much, because no despair of ours can alter the reality of things, or stain the joy of the cosmic dance which is always there. Indeed, we are in the midst of it, and it is in the midst of us, for it beats in our very blood, whether we want it to or not.

Yet the fact remains that we are invited to forget ourselves on purpose, cast our awful solemnity to the winds and join in the general dance.